Kindle Fire

FOR

DUMMIES®

Kindle Fire™ FOR DUMMIES®

by Nancy C. Muir

WILEY

John Wiley & Sons, Inc.

Kindle Fire™ For Dummies®

Published by
John Wiley & Sons, Inc.
111 River Street
Hoboken, NJ 07030-5774

www.wiley.com

Copyright © 2012 by John Wiley & Sons, Inc., Hoboken, New Jersey

Published by John Wiley & Sons, Inc., Hoboken, New Jersey

Published simultaneously in Canada

For general information on our other products and services, please contact our Customer Care Department within the U.S. at 877-762-2974, outside the U.S. at 317-572-3993, or fax 317-572-4002.

For technical support, please visit www.wiley.com/techsupport.

Wiley publishes in a variety of print and electronic formats and by print-on-demand. Some material included with standard print versions of this book may not be included in e-books or in print-on-demand. If this book refers to media such as a CD or DVD that is not included in the version you purchased, you may download this material at http://booksupport.wiley.com. For more information about Wiley products, visit www.wiley.com.

ISBN 978-1-118-26788-2 (paper); ISBN 978-1-118-16163-0 (mobi ebook); ISBN 978-1-118-27197-1 (e-PDF)

Manufactured in the United States of America

10 9 8 7 6 5 4 3 2 1

WILEY

About the Author

Nancy C. Muir: Nancy Muir is the author of almost 100 technology books on topics ranging from tablet computers and popular computer applications to nanotechnology. Her website TechSmart Senior (www.techsmartsenior.com) provides information for those reading her bestselling *Computers for Seniors For Dummies* and *Laptops for Seniors For Dummies* books (both published by Wiley) and others discovering technology later in their lives. She is the senior editor for Understanding Nano (www.understandingnano.com), a website that provides articles and information about nanotechnology. Prior to her writing career, Nancy was a manager in both the publishing and computer software industries.

Dedication

To Starfire.

Author's Acknowledgments

I could not have written this book without the help and support of my wonderful husband, Earl Boysen. Earl helped me in some very practical ways by performing research and doing the tech edit on this book. In addition, I must thank Katie Mohr, Acquisitions Editor extraordinaire, who jumped through many hoops to make this book happen and had faith in my ability to write this book. Laura Miller performed heroic editorial feats by making my words sound literate on a very fast-paced schedule. Finally, I'd like to thank Kevin Molloy of Amazon for his help in providing information and advice about Kindle Fire so that my readers can get the most out of their Kindle Fires.

Publisher's Acknowledgments

We're proud of this book; please send us your comments at http://dummies.custhelp.com. For other comments, please contact our Customer Care Department within the U.S. at 877-762-2974, outside the U.S. at 317-572-3993, or fax 317-572-4002.

Some of the people who helped bring this book to market include the following:

Acquisitions and Editorial

Project Editor: Laura K. Miller

Sr. Acquisitions Editor: Katie Mohr

Copy Editor: Laura K. Miller

Technical Editor: Earl Boysen

Editorial Manager: Jodi Jensen

Editorial Assistant: Amanda Graham

Sr. Editorial Assistant: Cherie Case

Photographers: Michael Trent, Kevin Kirschner

Cover Photo: © iStockphoto.com/fleag (background); image of device by Michael Trent

Composition Services

Project Coordinator: Kristie Rees

Layout and Graphics: Samantha K. Cherolis, Lavonne Roberts, Brent Savage

Proofreaders: Laura Albert, Betty Kish, Susan Moritz

Indexer: Steve Rath

All Gallery photos: Courtesy of Ashley Ernstberger Photography

Additional cover images: Angry Birds Free — Rovio Entertainment, Ltd. ESPN ScoreCenter — ESPN, Inc. Basic Spanish For Dummies — Skava

---

Publishing and Editorial for Technology Dummies

    Richard Swadley, Vice President and Executive Group Publisher

    Andy Cummings, Vice President and Publisher

    Mary Bednarek, Executive Acquisitions Director

    Mary C. Corder, Editorial Director

Publishing for Consumer Dummies

    Kathleen Nebenhaus, Vice President and Executive Publisher

Composition Services

    Debbie Stailey, Director of Composition Services

Contents at a Glance

Table of Contents

Introduction

Kindle Fire is a very affordable way to get at all kinds of media, from music and videos to books and colorful magazines. It's also a device that allows you to browse the Internet, check your e-mail, and read documents. Its portability makes it incredibly useful for people on the go in today's fast-paced world.

In this book, I introduce you to all the cool features of Kindle Fire, providing tips and advice for getting the most out of this ingenious little tablet. I help you find your way around its attractive and easy-to-use interface, and even recommend some neat apps that make your device more functional and fun.

Why Buy This Book?

"If Kindle Fire is so easy to use, why do I need a book?" you may be asking yourself. When I first sat down with Kindle Fire, it took about three or four days of poking around to find settings, features, and ways to buy and locate my content and apps. When was the last time you had four days to spare? I've spent the time so that you can quickly and easily get the hang of all the Kindle Fire features and discover a few tricks I bet your friends won't uncover for quite a while.

Foolish Assumptions

You may have opted for a tablet to watch movies and read books on the run. You might think it's a good way to browse business documents and check e-mail on your next plane trip. You might have one or more computers and be very computer savvy, or you might hate computers and figure that Kindle Fire gives you all the computing power you need to browse the Internet and read e-books.

Kindle Fire users come in all types. I won't assume in this book that you're a computer whiz, but I will assume that you have a passing understanding of how to copy a file and plug in a USB cable. I'm guessing you've browsed the Internet at least a few times and heard of Wi-Fi, which is what you use to go online with a Kindle Fire. Other than that, you don't need a lot of technical background to get the most out of this book.

How This Book Is Organized

For Dummies books don't require a linear read, meaning that you could jump in anywhere and find out what you need to know about a particular feature. However, if you're opening the box and starting from square one with your Kindle Fire, consider working through the first couple of chapters first. They provide information about setting up your Kindle Fire and navigating your way around its interface.

Subsequent chapters help you go online and set up your e-mail account, and then begin to explore the wealth of multimedia and written content Kindle Fire makes available to you. I even include two chapters at the end of the book that recommend apps you can get to add basic functionality to the Kindle Fire, such as a calendar and notes, and ten games to turn your Kindle Fire into a great gaming machine.

Icons Used in This Book

Icons are little pictures in the margin of this book that alert you to special types of advice or information, including

These short words of advice draw your attention to faster, easier, or alternative ways of getting things done with Kindle Fire.

When you see this icon, you'll know that I'm emphasizing important information for you to keep in mind as you use a feature.

There aren't too many ways you can get in trouble with the Kindle Fire, but in those few situations where some action might be irreversible, I include warnings so you avoid any pitfalls

Get Going!

Time to get that Kindle Fire out of its box, set it up, and get going with all the fun, entertaining things it makes available to you. Have fun!

Chapter 1

Overview of the Kindle Fire

In This Chapter

▶ Comparing Kindle Fire to the competition

▶ Surveying all of the Kindle Fire's features

Amazon, the giant online retailer, just happens to have access to more content (music, movies, audio books, and so on) than just about anybody on the planet. So, when an Amazon tablet was rumored to be in the works, and as Amazon stacked up media partnerships with the likes of Fox and PBS, the mystery tablet was seen as the first real challenge to Apple's iPad.

Now, the Kindle Fire is available, and it turns out to be an awesome machine in its own right, one that provides the right price and feature mix for many people, while offering the key to that treasure chest of content Amazon has been wise enough to amass.

In this chapter, you get an overview of the Kindle Fire: how it compares to competing devices and its key features.

How Kindle Fire Stacks Up to the Competition

Let's start at the beginning. A *tablet* is a handheld computer with an onscreen keyboard and apps that allow you to play games, read e-books, check e-mail, browse the web, and more.

In the world of tablets, the first device to hit big was iPad, and then subsequent tablets, such as Samsung Galaxy and HP TouchPad, appeared. No tablet since iPad seems to have gained a foothold in the market up to now, so the logical comparison here is to the iPad.

Kindle Fire is lighter and smaller than iPad, sporting a 7-inch display (see Figure 1-1) and weighing only 14.6 ounces, versus iPad's 9.7-inch display and 1.3-pound frame. That smaller, lighter form factor makes the Kindle Fire easier to hold with one hand than the iPad.

Kindle Fire has a projected battery life of eight hours, versus iPad's ten hours, but those two hours are a result of a lighter-weight battery (and therefore, a lighter device), which is probably a fair trade-off for most. The screen resolution on the Kindle Fire's bright color screen is just about on par with the iPad screen.

Figure 1-1:
The neat size and weight of Kindle Fire make it easy to hold.

Kindle Fire has 8GB of internal storage, versus 16, 32, or 64GB on the various iPad models, but there's a reason for that. Amazon provides free storage for all your Amazon-purchased content in the *Cloud* (a huge collection of online storage) so that you can stream video and music instead of downloading it, if you like.

Kindle Fire also has some very intelligent technology that allows your browser to take advantage of the Cloud to display your web pages faster.

In its first generation model, Kindle Fire has no cameras and no microphone, which means you can't take pictures or make phone calls by using it.

Table 1-1 provides an at-a-glance view of Kindle Fire features.

Table 1-1	Kindle Fire Specifications
Feature	*Kindle Fire Specs*
Display size	7 in.
Processor	Dual Core
Screen resolution	1024 × 600
Internal storage	8GB
Battery life	8 hours
Price	$199
Content	Amazon Appstore
Connectivity	Wi-Fi
Ports	USB 2.0
Browser	Silk
Camera	None

In several ways, Kindle Fire is easy to use, with a simple Android-based touchscreen interface, and it's a great device for consuming media — and what a lot of media Amazon makes available! Kindle Fire also offers a brand new browser named Silk, an e-mail client, and the fabulous Kindle e-reader (see Figure 1-2). So, despite the lack of cameras, a microphone, and a few pre-installed apps such as a calendar and calculator (which you can buy from the Amazon Appstore), with its dramatically lower price point, Kindle Fire may be the tablet of choice for many.

Just because a particular type of app doesn't come preinstalled doesn't mean you can't get one, often for free. At this point, the selection of apps available for Android devices isn't nearly as robust as those available for Apple devices, but that will change over time. See Chapter 10 for a list of ten apps that can flesh out your Kindle Fire with popular features such as a budget tracker, calendar, weather reporter, and calculator, and check out Chapter 11 for ten or so great game apps.

Figure 1-2:
Where it
all started,
with Kindle
e-reader
functionality.

Key Features of Kindle Fire

Kindle Fire is one spiffy little device with all the things most people want from a tablet packed into an easy-to-hold package: e-mail, web browsing, players for video and music content, an e-reader, a great online content store, access to tens of thousands of Android apps, and so on. In the following sections, you get to explore all these great features.

Check out the price

In case you didn't notice in the overview of features in the section "How Kindle Fire Stacks Up to the Competition," earlier in this chapter, Kindle Fire costs much less than the lowest priced iPad: $199 versus $499.

'Nuff said?

Just keep in mind that at the top end, you'll pay $829 for a 64GB 3G iPad. Granted, Kindle Fire doesn't offer a 3G option and has less memory; but although it's inexpensive, it's a very well-made device. How does Amazon offer a quality device at this low a price? Quite simply, they're making a bet that they'll make up in content sales what they lose on the cost of the hardware. And you, the consumer, are the winner!

Pre-installed functionality

Here's a rundown of the functionality you get out of the box from pre-installed apps:

- E-reader to read both books and periodicals
- Music player
- Video player
- Contacts app
- Document reader for Word, PDF, RTF, and HTML format files
- Silk web browser
- Gallery (see Figure 1-3) in which you can view and make a very few edits (rotate and crop) to photos
- E-mail client (meaning you can set up Kindle Fire to access your existing e-mail accounts)

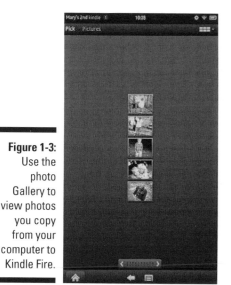

Figure 1-3: Use the photo Gallery to view photos you copy from your computer to Kindle Fire.

Photos used by permission of Ashley Ernstberger Photography

There is a free version of Quickoffice that comes pre-installed on your Kindle Fire. This app offers a mini-suite of productivity products, including a word processor, spreadsheet, and presentation software.

Kindle Fire gives you the ability to

- ✔ Shop at Amazon for music, video, apps, books, and periodicals.
- ✔ Store Amazon-purchased content in the Amazon Cloud and play music and video selections from the Cloud, instead of downloading them to your device.
- ✔ Send documents to yourself at a Kindle e-mail address that's assigned when you register your device.
- ✔ Sideload content from your computer to your Kindle Fire by using a micro-B cable that you can purchase separately. Using this cable (see Figure 1-4), you can copy photos, music, videos, and documents (Word or PDF) from any source onto your Kindle Fire.

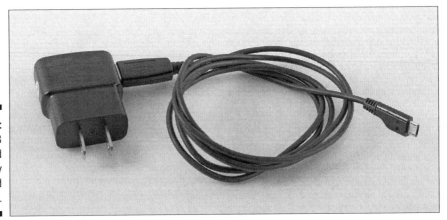

Figure 1-4:
The micro-B cable, sold separately for around $10.

The magic of Whispersync

If you've ever owned a Kindle e-reader, you know that downloading content to it has always been seamless. All you need for this process is access to a Wi-Fi network. Then, you simply order a book, and within moments, it appears on your Kindle device.

Kindle Fire enjoys the same kind of easy download capability via Amazon's Whispersync technology for books, music, video, and periodicals.

Whispersync also helps sync items such as bookmarks you've placed in e-books or the last place you watched in a video across various devices. For example, say you have the Kindle e-reader app on your Kindle Fire, PC, and smartphone. Wherever you left off reading, whatever notes you entered, and whatever pages you've bookmarked will be synced among all the devices without you having to lift a finger.

Content, content, content!

Kindle Fire is meant as a device you use to consume media, meaning that you can play/read all kinds of music, movies, TV shows, podcasts, e-books, magazines, and newspapers. As I mention in the section "How Kindle Fire Stacks Up to the Competition," earlier in this chapter, Amazon has built up a huge amount of content, from print and audio books (1 million titles and counting in the Kindle Store, shown in Figure 1-5) to movies and TV shows (100,000 movies and TV series), music (17 million songs), and hundreds of your favorite magazines. Count on these numbers to have risen by the time you read this: Amazon continues to rack up deals with media groups such as Fox Broadcasting and PBS to make even more content available on a regular basis.

You can find various kinds of content in the Amazon store by clicking the Store button in the libraries that you access through the Kindle Fire Home screen. Tap Newsstand to shop for periodicals (see Figure 1-6) and Music to shop for songs and albums, tap Video to go directly to the Amazon VideoStore, and tap Apps to shop the Amazon Appstore. All the content you purchase is backed up on the Amazon Cloud.

Figure 1-5:
The Kindle Store offers more than 1 million books for the Kindle e-reader app.

Figure 1-6:
Amazon's
magazine
selection is
constantly
growing.

See Chapter 6 for more about buying content and apps for your Kindle Fire.

The ability to quickly and easily access all this content and play it back or display it on your Kindle Fire is probably the main reason why this great little device is a tablet game changer.

You can also transfer documents from your computer or send them via e-mail and read them on Kindle Fire. Note that docs are not backed up in the Amazon Cloud.

Browsing with Amazon Silk

Silk is Amazon's new browser (see Figure 1-7). Silk is simple to use, but the real benefits of Amazon Silk are all about browsing performance.

Amazon Silk is touted as a "Cloud-accelerated split browser." In plain English, this means that the browser can use the power of Amazon's servers to load the pages of a website quickly. Because parts of the process of loading web pages are handled not on Kindle Fire, but on servers in the Cloud, your pages simply display faster.

Figure 1-7:
Amazon
Silk offers
simple-
to-use
browsing
tools.

In addition, you get what's called a persistent connection, which means that your tablet is always connected to the Amazon Internet backbone (the routes that data travels to move among networks online) whenever it has access to a Wi-Fi connection.

Another fascinating ability of Silk is the way it filters content to deliver it faster. Say you open a news site, such as MSN or CNN. Obviously, millions of others are accessing these pages on the same day. If most of those folks choose to open the Entertainment page after reading the home page of the site, Silk essentially predicts what page you might open next and pre-loads it. If you choose to go to that page, too, it appears instantly.

But is it private?

There were some early misgivings about privacy and the Silk browser. Folks were concerned about the fact that Amazon collects information about browsing habits in order to predict what page most folks were likely to browse to next.

These fears were allayed when Amazon assured the press and others that they don't collect personally identifiable information (meaning they note that a user clicked a particular link but don't keep a record of which user did so), nor do they use this information for anything other than to produce a better browsing experience.

Taking advantage of free Cloud storage

In the section "How Kindle Fire Stacks Up to the Competition," earlier in this chapter, I mention that Kindle Fire has less storage space (8GB) than some competing tablets. That amount of storage will probably work just fine for you because when you own a Kindle Fire, you get free, unlimited Cloud storage for all digital content purchased from Amazon (but not content that you copy onto Kindle Fire from your computer by using a micro-B cable). This means that books, movies, music, and apps are held online for you to stream or download at any time, instead of being stored on your Kindle Fire.

This storage means that you don't use up your Kindle Fire memory. As long as you have a Wi-Fi connection, you can stream content from Amazon's Cloud at anytime. If you'll be away from a connection, download an item (such as an episode of your favorite TV show) and watch it, and then remove it from your device the next time you're within range of a Wi-Fi network. The content is still available in the Cloud: You can download that content again or stream it anytime you like.

A world of color on the durable display

The display on Kindle Fire offers 16 million colors (see Figure 1-8). The high-resolution screen makes for very crisp colors when you're watching that hit movie or reading a colorful magazine. *In-plane switching* is a technology that gives you a wide viewing angle on the Kindle Fire screen. The result is that, if you want to share your movie with a friend sitting next to you on the couch, she'll have no problem seeing what's on the screen from that side angle.

Figure 1-8:
The bright
display
on Kindle
Fire makes
media shine.

In addition, the glass screen is coated with layers that make it extra strong — 30 times harder than plastic — so it should withstand most of the bumps and scratches you throw at it.

Of course, you should avoid dropping your Kindle Fire, exposing it to extreme temperatures, or spilling liquids on it. The User Guide also advises that, if you do spill liquids, you shouldn't heat the device in your microwave to dry it off. (Perhaps a case of tablet maintenance advice for real dummies?)

Note that Kindle Fire, although it has a screen that renders images crisply, is not a high-definition device. Although you can purchase and play HD versions of movies and TV shows, they'll play just like non-HD media. See Chapter 8 for more about playing video content.

Understanding the value of Amazon Prime

Kindle Fire comes with one free month of Amazon Prime. I've been an Amazon Prime member for years, so I can tell you firsthand that this service is one of the best deals out there. During your free month, Prime will allow you to get a lot of perks, such as free two-day shipping on thousands of items sold through Amazon and free instant videos.

If you decide to pick up the service after your free month, it will cost you $79 a year. So, what do you get for your money?

Prime includes free two-day shipping on millions of items and overnight shipping for only $3.99. Not every item offered on Amazon is eligible for Prime, but enough are that it's a wonderful savings in time and money over the course of a year. You can probably pay for the membership with the free shipping on the first two or three orders you place. And getting your Prime stuff in only two days every time is sweet.

In addition, Prime membership gives you access to Prime Instant Videos (see Figure 1-9), which includes thousands of movies and TV shows that can be streamed to your Kindle Fire absolutely free. We're not talking obscure 1970s sleepers, here: Recent additions to Prime Instant Videos include TV shows such as all the *Star Trek* series and the hit series *Frasier,* and award winning movies such as *Elizabeth* and *Notting Hill.*

Figure 1-9:
The Prime
Instant
Videos
service
adds new
videos all
the time;
check it out!

If you already have a paid Amazon Prime account, you don't get an extra month for free, sad to say. And if you don't have a Prime account, your 30 days of a free account starts from the time you activate your Kindle Fire, not the first time you make a Prime purchase or stream a Prime Instant Video. So, my suggestion is to start using it right away to take full advantage and decide whether the paid membership is for you.

Chapter 2

Kindle Fire Quickstart

*T*he basics of using Kindle are . . . well, pretty basic. You start by turning it on and following a set of extremely short and simple instructions to set it up and register it, and then you can start to get acquainted with its features.

In this chapter, I help you to get familiar with what comes in the box, explore the interface (what you see on the screen), and start to use your fingers to interact with the touchscreen. Finally, to round out your introduction to Kindle Fire basics, you can begin to get a sense of how things are organized on Kindle Fire's Home screen.

Get Going with Kindle Fire

There's always a logical place to start building a fire. In this case, forget the logs and matches, and get started by examining what comes in the Kindle Fire box and learn how to turn your nifty new device on and off. The first time you turn on Kindle Fire, you register it and link it to your Amazon account so that you can shop till you drop.

Also, although your device probably comes with a decent battery charge, at some point, you'll inevitably have to charge the battery, so I cover that in the section "Charging the battery," later in this chapter, as well.

Opening the box

When your Kindle Fire arrives, it will come in a plain brown box (see Figure 2-1). The Kindle Fire itself rests on top of a piece of hard plastic, and a small brown card with some Kindle Fire basics printed on both sides is slotted into the lid of the box. Finally, beneath the piece of plastic rests a charger in a paper sleeve. That's it.

Remove the protective plastic from the device, and you're ready to get going.

Figure 2-1:
The
Kindle Fire
packaging.

Turning your Kindle Fire on and off

After you get the tablet out of its packaging, it's time to turn it on. The Kindle Fire sports a Power button on the bottom of the device when you hold it in portrait orientation (see Figure 2-2). Next to the Power button is a port where you can insert a micro-B cable to connect the Kindle Fire to your computer, as well as a headphone jack.

To turn the device on, press the Power button. If you're starting up for the first time, you're taken through a series of setup screens (see the following section for more about this). After you go through the setup process and register your Kindle Fire, you'll see the Home screen shown in Figure 2-3 on startup. The Status Bar gives you information about items such as your device's battery charge, as well as access to a Quick Settings menu for universal Kindle Fire settings; the Options bar at the bottom of the screen provides access to settings and tools that are context-specific (they vary depending on what you're doing at the time). You can find more about the elements on the Home screen in the section "Getting to Know the Interface," later in this chapter.

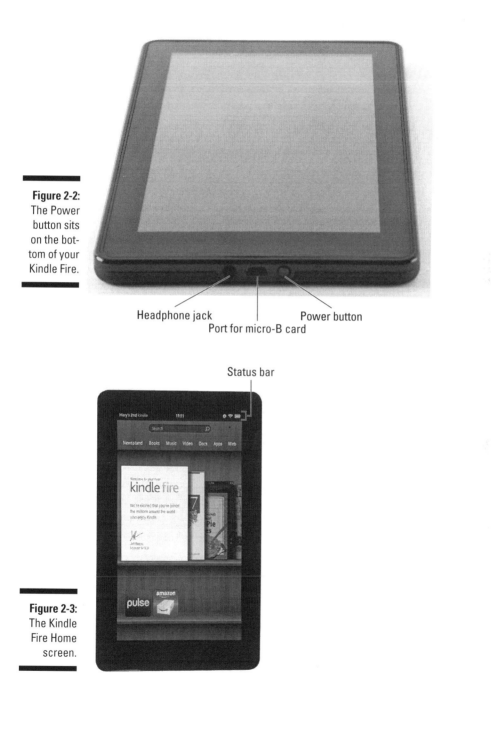

Figure 2-2:
The Power button sits on the bottom of your Kindle Fire.

Headphone jack

Port for micro-B card

Power button

Status bar

Figure 2-3:
The Kindle Fire Home screen.

If you want to lock your Kindle Fire, which is akin to putting a laptop computer to sleep, tap the Power button again. To shut down your Kindle, press and hold the Power button until a message appears offering you the options to Shut Down or Cancel, as shown in Figure 2-4.

Figure 2-4:
You can proceed to shut down your device, or cancel and return to the Home screen.

If your Kindle Fire becomes non-responsive, you can press and hold the Power button for 20 seconds, and it should come to life again.

If you place the device on a surface such as a table oriented with the Power button on the bottom, perhaps to show a friend or client something on the screen, you can accidentally hit the Power button and send Kindle Fire to sleep.

Getting to know the touchscreen

Before you work through the setup screens for your Kindle Fire, it will help if you to get to know the basics of navigating the touchscreen — especially if you've never used a touchscreen before:

- ✔ Tap an item to select it or double-tap an item (such as an app) to open it.
- ✔ If your Kindle Fire goes to a lock screen after a period of inactivity, swipe your finger from right to left across the yellow band that has an arrow on one end (see Figure 2-5) to go to the Home screen.

Arrow

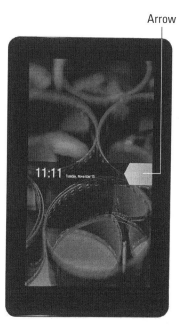

11:11 Tuesday, November 15

Figure 2-5:
Swipe this
arrow to go
to the Home
screen.

> ✔ Double-tap to enlarge text and double-tap again to return the text to its
> original size. Note, this works only in certain locations, such as when
> displaying a web page in the Silk browser.
>
> ✔ Place your fingers apart on a screen and pinch them together to zoom in
> on the current view; place your fingers together on the screen and then
> move them apart (unpinch) to enlarge the view.
>
> ✔ Swipe left to move to the next page in apps such as the e-reader or the
> Silk web browser. Swipe to the right to move to the previous page.
>
> ✔ Swipe up and down to scroll up and down a web page.

These touchscreen gestures will help you get around most of the content and
setup screens you encounter in Kindle Fire.

Setting up your Kindle Fire

When you turn Kindle Fire on for the first time, you see a series of screens
that help you set up and register the device. Don't worry: There aren't many
questions, and you know all the answers.

The first screen is titled Welcome to Kindle Fire. This is the point in the setup process at which you connect to a Wi-Fi network. You need this connection to register your device.

At some point during this setup procedure you may be prompted to plug your adapter in, if your battery charge is low. You may also be notified that the latest Kindle software is downloading and have to wait for that process to complete before you can move forward.

Follow these steps to register and set up your Kindle Fire:

1. **In the Connect to a Network list (shown on the screen in Figure 2-6), tap an available network.**

   Kindle Fire connects to the network (you may need to enter a password and then tap Connect to access an available network) and then displays the Time Zone screen (see Figure 2-7).

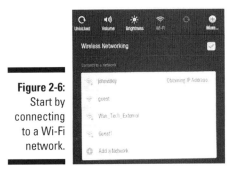

Figure 2-6: Start by connecting to a Wi-Fi network.

2. **Tap to select a time zone from the list provided.**

   For countries other than the United States, tap More and choose from the provided list. After you select from the list, tap the Back button in the bottom-left corner to return to the Time Zone screen.

3. **Tap Continue.**

4. **On the Register Your Kindle screen that appears (see Figure 2-8), enter your Amazon account information, e-mail address, and a password in the appropriate fields; then skip to Step 7.**

   See Step 5 if you don't have an Amazon account.

   You can choose to deselect the Show Password checkbox so that your password doesn't appear on your screen as you type it. This protects your password from prying eyes.

Figure 2-7:
Choose your
time zone.

Figure 2-8:
Register
your Kindle
Fire to use it.

5. **If you don't have an Amazon account, click the New to Amazon? Create an Account link.**

   This link takes you to the Create an Amazon Account screen (see Figure 2-9), with fields for entering your name, e-mail address, and password (which you have to retype to confirm).

6. **Enter this information, and then tap Continue.**

Figure 2-9:
The Create an Amazon Account screen.

7. **If you want to read the terms of registration, tap the By Registering, You Agree to All of the Terms Found Here link.**

8. **When you finish reading the terms, tap the Close button to return to the registration screen.**

9. **To complete the registration, tap the Register button.**

   A final screen appears saying Welcome to Kindle Fire: Hello <*Your Name*>. There's also a link labeled Not <*Your Name*>? If, for some reason, you aren't you (for example, you may have entered your account information incorrectly), tap the Not <*Your Name*> link to change your account information.

This is probably the point at which the Kindle Fire may download the latest Kindle software. If so, sit back, relax, and anticipate using your new toy.

When the download finishes, tap the Get Started Now button, and you can view a series of quick tips to get you started with Kindle Fire, as shown in Figure 2-10. (If you need more help at any time, you can refer to the User's Guide in the Kindle Fire Docs library.) Tap Next to move through this tour; on the last of the three screens, tap Close to get going with Kindle Fire.

Figure 2-10:
This very quick tutorial covers the basics of using Kindle Fire.

Charging the battery

Kindle Fire has a battery life of seven-and-a-half hours for Wi-Fi–connected activities, such as web browsing, streaming movies, and listening to music from the Cloud. If you're a bookworm who's more into the printed word than media, you'll be happy to hear that you get about eight-and-a-half hours of reading downloaded books with wireless turned off.

You charge the battery by using the provided charger. Attach the smaller end of the charger to your Kindle Fire's micro-B port, located near the Power button, and the other end to a wall outlet. If Kindle Fire is completely out of juice, it will take about four hours to charge it.

There's a battery indicator on the Status bar that runs across the top of the Kindle Fire screen that you can check to see if your battery is running low.

Getting to Know the Interface

The interface you see on the Kindle Home screen (see Figure 2-11) is made up of three areas. At the top, you see a set of buttons that take you to the Kindle Fire libraries that contain various types of content. In the middle of the screen is the Carousel. The Carousel contains images of items you recently used that you can flick with your finger to scroll through and tap to open. Finally, the bottom portion of the Home screen contains items you've saved to your Favorites (plus a few items Amazon pre-saved there for you).

Carousel

Library buttons

Figure 2-11: This graphical interface is fun to move around with the flick of a finger.

Favorites

Understanding the Cloud and Kindle Fire

Everything you buy using Kindle Fire is purchased through Amazon or its affiliates on the Amazon site. That content is downloaded to your device through a technology called Whispersync, which requires a Wi-Fi connection.

You can choose when you purchase content whether to keep it in the Amazon Cloud or download it to your Kindle Fire. If you download

it, you can access it whether or not you're in range of a Wi-Fi network. At any time, you can remove content from the device, and it will be archived in the Cloud for you to stream to your device (music or video) or re-download (music, video, books, and magazines) anytime you like.

Accessing Kindle Fire libraries

Kindle Fire libraries are where you access downloaded content, as well as content stored by Amazon in the Cloud. Libraries (with the exception of the Docs library) also offer a Store button that you can tap to go online to browse and buy more content.

Tap any library button to open a library of downloaded and archived content: Newsstand, Books, Music, Video, or Apps. Note that there's also a Docs button, where documents that you sideload from your computer or receive as e-mail attachments in your Kindle inbox are placed.

The Video app opens to the Amazon store, rather than a library, because in most cases, it's not very prudent to download video content to your Kindle Fire. Because this type of content takes up so much of your memory, it's preferable to play video from Amazon's Cloud (which is called *streaming*).

There's also a Web button at the far right that you can tap to open the Silk web browser. Find out more about going online and using the browser in Chapter 5.

In a library, such as the Music library shown in Figure 2-12, you can tap the Device or Cloud tab. The Device tab shows you only content you have downloaded; the Cloud tab displays all your purchases or free content stored in Amazon's Cloud library, including content you've downloaded to the Kindle Fire.

You can download archived content at any time or remove downloaded content to the Cloud. You can also view the contents of libraries in different ways, depending on which library you're in. For example, you can view Music library contents by categories such as Songs, Artists, and Albums.

When you go to a library and tap the Cloud button, content that's not currently downloaded sports a little downloading arrow in the bottom-right corner. You can re-download that content by tapping the item at any time.

Figure 2-12:
Your Music library provides access to all your musical content.

See Chapter 4 for more about buying content, Chapter 6 for information about reading books and magazines, and Chapters 7 and 8 for more about playing music and video.

It's possible to download video, which is useful if you'll be out of range of a Wi-Fi connection, but I recommend you remove the content from your device when you're done watching and back in Wi-Fi range. Removing content from Kindle Fire involves pressing it with your finger and choosing Remove from Device from the menu that appears.

As mentioned before, you can also sideload content you've obtained from other sources, such as iTunes, to your Kindle Fire libraries. Sideloading involves purchasing a micro-B cable (about $10 from Amazon but also available from other sources), and then using the cord to connect Kindle Fire to your computer and copy content to Kindle Fire. See the section "Using a Micro-B Cable to Transfer Data," later in this chapter, for more about this process.

Playing with the Carousel

Many of us have fond memories of riding a carousel at the fair as kids. The Kindle Fire Carousel may not bring the same thrill, but it does have its charms as you swipe through it to see a revolving display of recent books, music, videos, websites, docs, and apps (see Figure 2-13).

Figure 2-13:
Kindle Fire's
Carousel
makes
recently
used
content
available.

If you've used an Android device, such as a smartphone, you've probably encountered the Carousel concept. On Kindle Fire, items you've used recently are displayed here chronologically, with the most recent item you used on top. You can swipe your finger to the right or left to flick through the Carousel contents. When you find an item you want to view or play, tap to open it.

Whatever you tap opens in the associated player or reader. Music will open in the Amazon MP3 music player; video in the Amazon Video player; and docs, books, and magazines in the Kindle e-reader.

When you first begin using Kindle Fire, before you've accessed any content, by default the Carousel contains the Amazon Kindle User Guide and the absolutely free New Oxford American Dictionary. It may also contain recently used content from your Amazon Cloud library.

Organizing Favorites

When you're on a roll using Kindle Fire for accessing all kinds of content, the Carousel can get a bit crowded. You may have to swipe five or six times to find what you need. That's where Favorites comes in.

The concept of Favorites is probably familiar to you from working with web browsers, in which Favorites is a feature that allows you to put websites you visit frequently in a Favorites folder. On the Kindle Fire, Favorites is also a place for saving frequently used content which takes the form of a virtual bookcase.

If, for example, you're reading a book you open often or you play a certain piece of music frequently, place it in the Favorites area of the Kindle Fire Home screen, and you can find it more quickly.

By default, Favorites includes an Amazon Store app, Pulse (a news aggregator app), the IMDb movie database app, and the Facebook app. To pin an item to Favorites, press and hold it in the Carousel or a library, and then select Add to Favorites from the menu that appears (see Figure 2-14).

Figure 2-14: Pin items to Favorites by using this menu.

To remove content from Favorites, press and hold the item, and then choose Remove from Favorites or Delete from the menu that appears (see Figure 2-15). Remove from Favorites unpins the item from Favorites, although it's still available to you on the Carousel and in the related library. Delete removes the item from the device (although it's still archived in Amazon's Cloud).

Figure 2-15:
Use this menu to manage Favorites.

Getting clues from the Status bar

The Status bar runs across the top of every Kindle Fire screen, just like the Status bar on your mobile phone. This bar, shown in Figure 2-16, provides information about your battery charge and running apps, but it also provides access to the Kindle Fire settings.

Figure 2-16:
The various tools and settings available on the Status bar.

Mary's 2nd kindle 11:24

Here's a rundown of what you'll find on the Status bar:

- ✔ **Device name:** First is the name of your Kindle Fire, such as Nancy's Kindle or Nancy's 2nd Kindle.

- ✔ **Notifications:** A number sometimes appears next to the name of your device to indicate that you have that many Notifications. Notifications can come from the Kindle Fire system announcing a completed download or the e-mail client announcing that a new e-mail has arrived, for example. To view all your notifications, tap the Notifications icon, and a list appears (see Figure 2-17).

Notifications 2   Clear All

Downloads Completed
1 item downloaded

Import complete: katieeditor@yahoo.com 2:00 PM
Downloaded 67/Imported 4

- ✔ **Current time:** The next item on the Status bar is the current time, based on the time zone you specified when setting up the Kindle Fire.

- ✔ **Quick Settings:** Jumping to the right side of the Status bar, you first encounter a spoked-wheel-shaped icon that you tap to access Quick Settings. Quick Settings offer the most commonly used settings. Use these items to adjust volume, brightness, or your Wi-Fi connection, for example. To access the full Kindle Fire Settings menu, tap More (see Figure 2-18).

    See Chapter 3 for a detailed breakdown of all Kindle Fire settings.

- ✔ **Wi-Fi Connection:** The item on the Status bar to the right of Quick Settings is an icon showing you the Wi-Fi connection status. If this is lit up, you're connected. The more bars in the symbol that are bright white, the stronger the connection.

- ✔ **Battery charge:** Finally, there's an icon that indicates the percentage of charge remaining on your battery.

Figure 2-18:
Use the
Quick
Settings
menu or
tap More to
access the
full comple-
ment of
settings for
Kindle Fire.

The ever-present, ever-changing Options bar

The Options bar runs along the bottom of your Kindle Fire screen. The items offered on the Options bar change, depending on what library or app you're using, but they always include a Home button. Also, there are often items such as Search to run a search in features such as a content library. In addition, you'll almost always see a Menu button when you tap the Options bar. This icon makes available commonly used actions, such as those for accessing settings for the currently displayed feature. Figure 2-19 shows you the options available on the Music library screen.

Use the Home button to jump you back to the Kindle Fire from anywhere. On some screens where it would be annoying to be distracted by the Options bar, such as the e-reader, you may have to tap the bottom of the screen to make the Options bar appear.

Figure 2-19:
The Options
bar offers
contextually
relevant
options,
depending
on which
screen is
displayed.

Home button   Search

Menu button

Using a Micro-B Cable to Transfer Data

It's easy to purchase or rent content from Amazon, which you can choose to download directly to your Kindle Fire or stream from the Amazon Cloud. However, you may want to get content from other places, such as iTunes or your Pictures folder on your computer, and play or view it on your Kindle Fire.

To transfer content to Kindle Fire, you have to use a micro-B cable. This cable has a USB connector on one end that you can plug into your PC or Mac, and a micro-B connector on the other that fits into the slot on your Kindle Fire (which is located next to the Power button).

You can buy a micro-B cable from Amazon for about $10 or search for a cable from other sources, if you like (as long as there's a USB connector on one end and a micro-B connector on the other, it should work with your Kindle Fire).

When you get the cable, attach the micro-B end to your Kindle Fire (see Figure 2-20) and the USB end to your computer. Your Kindle Fire should then appear as a drive in Windows Explorer (see Figure 2-21) or the Mac Finder. You can now click and drag files from your hard drive to the Kindle Fire or use the copy and paste functions to accomplish the same thing.

Figure 2-20:
Connecting
the micro-B
cable to
Kindle Fire.

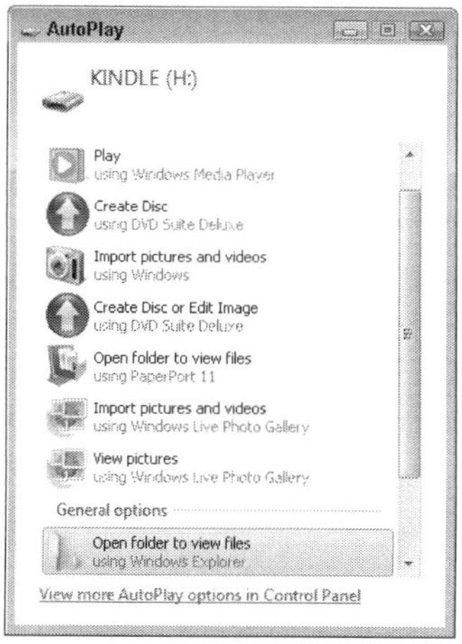

Figure 2-21:
Kindle Fire
contents
shown as
a drive in
Windows
Explorer.

Using this process, you can transfer apps, photos, docs, music, e-books, and videos from your computer to your Kindle Fire. Then, just tap the relevant library (such as Books for e-books and Music for songs) to read or play the content on your Kindle Fire.

You can also upload content to your Amazon Cloud library on your computer, and that content will then be available on your Kindle Fire from the Cloud. See Chapter 7 for more about how this process works.

Chapter 3

Kindle Fire Settings

* *

In This Chapter

▶ Opening your Kindle Fire's settings

▶ Working with Quick Settings

▶ Delving into all the settings Kindle Fire offers

* *

*W*hen you first take your Kindle Fire out of the box, Amazon has provided you with default settings that will work for most people most of the time. However, we've all gotten used to being able to personalize our experience with phone and computer devices, so you may be curious about the various ways in which you can make Kindle Fire work uniquely for you.

On a tablet device such as Kindle Fire, there are dozens of settings that help you manage your tablet experience. Some of these settings are discussed in the chapters that cover individual apps, such as the Amazon video player (Chapter 8) and Contacts (Chapter 9). But other settings are more general; I cover those more general settings in this chapter.

Opening Quick Settings

In this fast-paced day and age, quick is the name of the game for most of us, so Amazon has provided you with Quick Settings to streamline your settings experience.

You access both a short list of commonly used settings and all the more detailed settings for Kindle Fire by tapping the Quick Settings button in the Status bar. (This button looks like the spokes of a wheel and is located towards the top-right corner of the screen).

Here are the settings that you can control from the Quick Settings menu (see Figure 3-1):

Figure 3-1:
Quick
Settings
control the
settings that
you access
most often.

✔ **Unlocked/Lock:** This is a toggle feature, meaning that you tap it to lock your device, which displays a black screen, and then you tap the setting again to unlock it, which displays the Home screen.

✔ **Volume:** Tap Volume to display a slider bar that you can use to increase or decrease the volume (see Figure 3-2).

Figure 3-2:
Controls
that appear
when you
tap Volume.

✔ **Brightness:** You can tap and display Automatic Brightness On/Off buttons to turn on or off a feature that controls the brightness of the screen based on ambient light. You can also use the slider beneath this setting (see Figure 3-3) to adjust the brightness manually.

Figure 3-3:
Adjust
brightness
manually by
using this
slider.

✔ **Wi-Fi:** Tap to display an On/Off button (see Figure 3-4) that you can use to turn Wi-Fi on or off. When you turn Wi-Fi on, a list of available networks appears. Tap an available network to join it. Note that you may be asked to enter a password to access some networks.

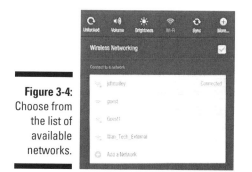

Figure 3-4:
Choose from
the list of
available
networks.

✔ **Sync:** Generally speaking, if you're within range of a Wi-Fi network, when you begin to download content, it downloads very quickly. However, if you've been out of range of a network, you might want to use this setting when you're back in range of a network to manually initiate the download of new content or continue downloads that may have been interrupted.

Finding Other Settings

Beyond what I discuss in the preceding section, there is one more item on the Quick Settings menu — More. Figure 3-5 shows you the many settings that appear when you tap the More button.

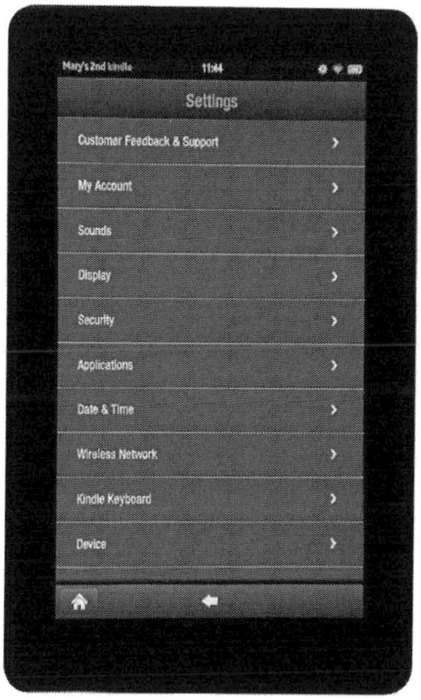

Figure 3-5:
Plenty more
settings are
revealed
when you
tap More.

These settings include: Customer Feedback & Support, My Account, Sounds, Display, Security, Applications, Date & Time, Wireless Network, Kindle Keyboard, Device, Legal Notices, and Terms of Use.

You won't need to change many of these settings very often because the way Kindle Fire works out of the box is usually very intuitive. But if you do find that you want to make an adjustment to settings such as the date and time, or security, it's useful to know what's available.

The following sections give you the skinny on what settings appear when you tap More in the Quick Settings menu.

Help & Feedback

Now and then, we all need a bit of help, and when you're first using a new device such as Kindle Fire, you should know where to find that help (on the off chance you don't have this book handy).

When you tap Customer Feedback & Support from Settings, you see the Help & Feedback screen, which offers a world of help and allows you to interact with Amazon customer service (see Figure 3-6).

Figure 3-6:
Help & Feedback settings for Kindle Fire.

The Help & Feedback screen includes three somewhat self-explanatory tabs: FAQ & Troubleshooting, Contact Customer Service, and Feedback. The last two tabs display a form in which you can type a message to send on to Amazon. Here's how these three options work:

✔ **FAQ & Troubleshooting:** Use this tab, shown in Figure 3-7, to get help with the following topics: Registration, Home Screen and Navigation, Books, Video, Docs, Web, Newsstand, and Other Apps. There is also a More Online Help link to connect you with additional Amazon resources.

Figure 3-7:
This Frequently Asked Questions tab leads you to help on a variety of topics.

✔ **Contact Customer Service:** The first question you have to answer here is "What can we help you with?" Use the Select an Issue drop-down list to locate a related issue and tap the Back button. You can also tap the Select Issue Details drop-down list, choose a more specific topic, and then tap the Back button. Choose from the How Would You Like to Contact Us field by selecting either e-mail (tap the Send Us an Email button) or phone (tap the Call Us button).

✔ **Feedback:** Tap Select a Feature and choose from the list that appears (items such as Newsstand, Books, Docs, and so on). Then, tap Back to go back to Feedback. Enter your comment in the Tell Us What You Think about This Feature field. You can also tap one to five stars to rate the feature you're providing feedback on (see Figure 3-8). Tap the Send Feedback button to submit your thoughts to Amazon.

Figure 3-8:
The
Feedback
tab of Help
& Feedback
gives you a
forum
for your
opinions.

My Account

Kindle Fire does much of what it does by accessing your Amazon account. You need to have an Amazon account to shop, access the Amazon Cloud library online, and register your Kindle Fire, for example.

The My Account option in Settings provides information about the account to which the device is registered (see Figure 3-9). To remove this account from your Kindle Fire, you can tap the Deregister button. Because the obvious thing to do next is to register your Kindle Fire to another account (because so much depends on your having an associated account), you then are presented with a Register button. Tap Register and fill in your Amazon username and password to register the device.

If you de-register your account, don't register your Kindle Fire, and leave this screen, you're placed in the introductory demo that appeared when you first set up your Kindle Fire. When you finish that demo and tap any category, such as Books, you're again prompted to register your device to your Amazon account.

Figure 3-9:
Check which
Amazon
account your
device is
registered to.

Controlling sounds

With a tablet that's so media-centric, accessing music and video, as well as games that you can play with their accompanying screeches and sounds, it's important that you know how to control the volume.

If you tap Sounds in Kindle Settings, you see two items (see Figure 3-10): a volume slider that you can use to move the volume up or down, and Notification Sounds. Notifications may come from the arrival of a new e-mail, a completed download, or an app notification (such as an appointment reminder from a calendar app that you may have downloaded). To modify Notification Sounds, tap the arrow on the right of this item and, from the list that appears, choose the sound you want to use.

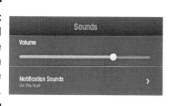

Figure 3-10:
Sound
settings are
pretty darn
simple
to use.

Managing the display

From within Settings, you can manage your device's display, adjusting both the screen brightness and how long it takes for the screen to lock when the device isn't being used.

Tap Display, and you can work with these settings (see Figure 3-11):

- ✓ **Brightness:** Tap and drag the circle on this slider to the right to make the screen brighter and to the left to dim it.

- ✓ **Screen Timeout:** After a certain period of inactivity, the Kindle Fire screen will lock and go black to save battery power. You can adjust the length of this interval by tapping the arrow in this field and choosing from a list that ranges from 30 seconds to one hour. You can also choose the option Never if you want your screen to be always on. However, remember that using the Never option or a very long interval will wear down your battery.

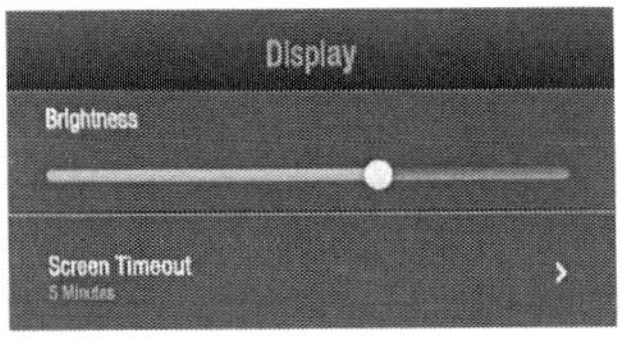

Figure 3-11: Manage display controls.

Making security settings

The first thing you can do to keep your Kindle Fire secure is to never let it out of your hands. But because we can't control everything and sometimes things get lost or stolen, it's a good idea to assign a password that's required to unlock your Kindle Fire screen. If a thief or other person gets his hands on your Kindle Fire, there's no way he can get at stored data, such as your Amazon account information or contacts.

Tap the Security Settings option, and you'll see three simple choices (see Figure 3-12):

- ✓ **Lock Screen Password On/Off:** Simply tap On, and fields appear labeled Enter Password and Confirm Password. Tap in the Enter Password field and, using the onscreen keyboard that appears, type a password. Tap in the Confirm Password field and retype the password. Tap Finish to save your new password.

- ✓ **Credential Storage:** Credentials are typically used for Microsoft Exchange–based accounts, such as an account you use to access e-mail on your company's server. If you use Microsoft Exchange, it's a good idea to get your network administrator's help to make the following settings: Install Secure Credentials, Set Credential Storage Password, Use Secure Credentials, and Clear Credential Storage.

▶ **Device Administrators:** If your device is being administered through a company Exchange account, use this setting to establish the device administrator who can modify settings for the account.

Figure 3-12:
The Security settings offer three ways to secure your Kindle Fire.

 You have to get an app if you want to set up Kindle Fire to work with Microsoft Exchange accounts. Try Exchange by Touchdown, which you can get from the Amazon Appstore by tapping Apps on your Home screen.

Working with applications

Apps can help you do everything from manage e-mail to play games. Managing the way apps work on your Kindle Fire is done through the Applications settings.

When you tap Applications in Settings, you see a list of installed apps, including the app that controls Settings (see Figure 3-13). Tap any of these apps, and you encounter the following options:

▶ **Force Stop:** Force Stop allows Kindle Fire to stop an application from running if it encounters problems.

▶ **Uninstall:** Uninstall removes the app from your Kindle Fire. Keep in mind, though, that although the app is uninstalled, if you purchased it from Amazon, it's still archived in the Cloud.

▶ **Storage:** You can clear Kindle Fire's memory of data stored by the app by tapping the Clear Data button.

▶ **Cache:** Computing devices store data based on your usage to more quickly provide the data you need. This so-called cache of data fills up a bit of memory, so if you want to free up some memory, tap the Clear Cache button.

✔ **Launch by Default:** Tap this button to launch an app automatically when you turn on Kindle Fire.

✔ **Permissions:** A list of permissions to allow access to information that this app might have to use to perform its function, such as your location.

Figure 3-13: Each application on your Kindle Fire has associated settings.

Adjusting date and time

You chose a Time Zone setting when you first set up your Kindle Fire (see Chapter 2). Your Kindle Fire uses the date and time setting to display the time in the Status bar, and also to work with other apps, such as a third-party calendar, for example. If you tap Date and Time in Settings, you see the four options shown in Figure 3-14:

✔ **Automatic:** If you want Kindle Fire to control the date and time based on your location, tap to turn this feature On. If you'd rather set the time manually, tap to turn this Off.

✔ **Set Time:** To manually set the time, after you turn the Automatic option Off, tap the arrow on the right of this setting to display additional settings (see Figure 3-15). Tap the + (plus sign) and – (minus sign) buttons to change the time, and then tap Save.

✔ **Set Date:** Tap the arrow to the right of Set Date and then tap the + (plus sign) and – (minus sign) buttons to set the date you want, and then tap Save.

✔ **Select Time Zone:** Tap the arrow to the right of this setting to change your time zone.

Figure 3-14: Let Kindle Fire control your time and date with the Automatic setting.

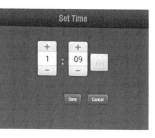

Figure 3-15: Manually set the time and date on your Kindle Fire.

The Set Time settings become available only if you first turn the Automatic option to Off.

Setting up Wi-Fi

Wi-Fi is a pretty essential setting for using Kindle Fire. Without a Wi-Fi connection, you can't stream video or music, shop at the various Amazon stores, or send and receive e-mail.

Tap Wireless Network to view the settings, shown in Figure 3-16:

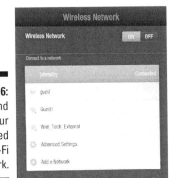

- ✔ **Wireless Network:** Turn Wi-Fi on or off. With Wi-Fi on, you can then click an item in the list of available networks, and Kindle connects to that network.

- ✔ **Add a Network:** Tap this setting to enter a new network's SSID (the public name of a Wi-Fi network) and security information to add it to the list of available networks.

- ✔ **Advanced Settings:** Tap this option to reveal settings that allow you to enable international channels (the options here are Europe or Japan) if you're travelling overseas and want to access foreign Wi-Fi networks; or modify static IP settings. Static IP settings are most relevant if you're trying to access a corporate network, in which case, your network administrator can probably give you the specific settings to use.

Working with the keyboard

There's no physical keyboard with your Kindle Fire, so you depend on its onscreen keyboard to provide input to apps such as Quickoffice, or in fields used to search and enter text into forms, such as e-mail messages.

There are three simple things you can do with Kindle Keyboard settings; all three offer the basic On/Off choices (see Figure 3-17):

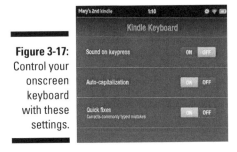

✔ **Sound on Keypress:** If you like that satisfying clicky sound when you tap a key on the onscreen keyboard, tap to turn this setting on.

✔ **Auto-Capitalization:** If you want Kindle Fire to automatically capitalize proper names or the first word in a sentence, tap to turn this setting on.

✔ **Quick Fixes:** Turning this setting on allows Kindle Fire to correct common typing errors, such as typing *teh* when you mean *the*.

Looking at device settings

You can check your Kindle Fire device settings (see Figure 3-18) to find out facts such as the remaining storage space available or your device's serial number. This is also where you can reset your Kindle Fire to the state it was in when it left the factory, if you like a clean slate now and then.

Figure 3-18: Device settings provide a lot of information about the status of your device.

Here are the device settings available to you:

✔ **Storage:** Tells you how much memory is still available on your device.

✔ **Battery:** Indicates the percentage of battery power remaining.

✔ **System Version:** Relates to the operating system version for your Kindle Fire. New versions are released periodically, so if your version isn't the most current, you might need to update it by tapping the Update Your Kindle button (see Figure 3-19).

Figure 3-19:
Amazon occasionally provides system updates; you can update manually.

System Version
Current Version: 6.1_user_2017120   Update your Kindle

✔ **Serial Number:** Here's where you can find the serial number you might need to reference to interact with Amazon technical or customer support.

✔ **Wi-Fi MAC Address:** Every device that can connect to a Wi-Fi network has a unique address. This is where you can find yours.

✔ **Allow Installation of Applications:** Kindle Fire is set up to get its content from Amazon because that provides some measure of confidence and security. For example, apps you sideload from your computer to Kindle Fire that are from third-party suppliers are more likely to introduce viruses to your computer. Still, you can buy apps elsewhere and port them over from your computer. If you want to allow this, choose On in this setting. If you don't want to let apps other than those verified by Amazon to be placed on your Kindle Fire, tap Off.

✔ **Reset to Factory Defaults:** This setting could come in handy in a couple of situations. If you sold your Kindle Fire to somebody (so you can buy a newer version, of course!), you wouldn't want that person to have your docs and contact information. Also, if you've loaded a lot of content on your Kindle Fire and then decide you want a clean beginning to clear up memory, you might choose to reset the device. Resetting wipes all content and any changes you've made to default settings. If you tap this setting, you see the confirming dialog box shown in Figure 3-20. Tap Erase Everything to continue with the reset procedure or Cancel to close the warning dialog box and halt the reset.

Figure 3-20:
Be sure
you want to
reset before
you accept
this option.

Although you get 8GB of storage with Kindle Fire, a chunk of that is taken up in pre-installed and system files. So the storage available may indicate that you have something like 6.5GB of total storage available on the device.

Chapter 4

Going Shopping!

*B*ecause Kindle Fire is, above all, a great device for consuming content, buying that content or downloading free content is a key step to enjoying it. Amazon offers both a rich supply of books, magazines, music, and video, and an Amazon Appstore that you can use to get your hands on apps that add to the functionality of your Kindle Fire. These apps can range from simple utilities such as a calculator to fun and addictive games and even a word processor or spreadsheet.

In this chapter, you can discover how to get apps, as well as books, magazines, music, and videos for your Kindle Fire.

Managing Your Amazon Account

You buy things from Amazon by using the account and payment information you provide when you create an Amazon account. You probably have an account if you ever bought anything on Amazon (or opened an account when you bought your Kindle Fire). To buy things on Amazon with your Kindle Fire, you need to have associated your Amazon account with your Kindle Fire, which happens during the setup process covered in Chapter 2 (see Figure 4-1).

After you associate your device with an Amazon account, you can manage account settings by going to the Amazon website by using the browser on either your Kindle Fire or computer, and then tapping or clicking (depending on whether you're using a touchscreen device) Your Account at the top-right of the Amazon screen (see Figure 4-2). You can then tap/click Manage Payment Options or Add a Credit or Debit Card from the Payment section of your account, and then change or enter a new method of payment and billing address.

Figure 4-1:
The screen
during setup
that asks
you to enter
account
information
or cre-
ate a new
account.

Your Account option

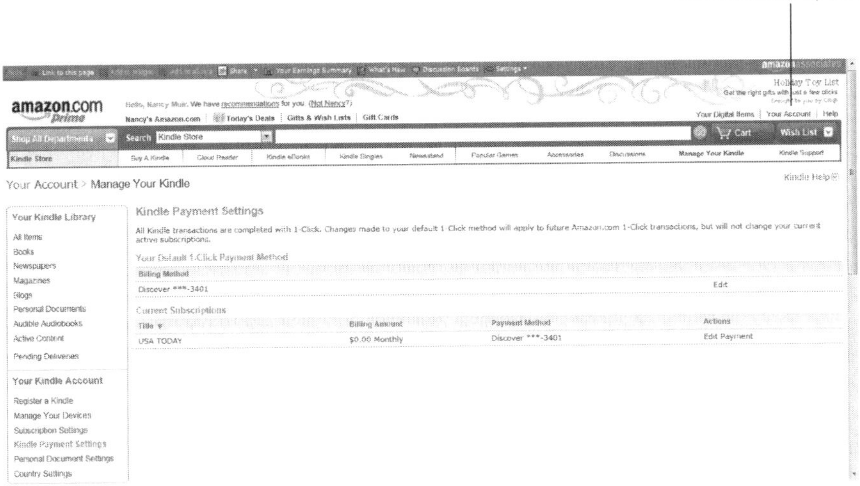

Figure 4-2:
Managing
your
Amazon
account on
a PC.

Visiting the Amazon Appstore

After you create an Amazon account (which I discuss in the preceding section), you can shop for all kinds of content from your Kindle Fire. I'll start by
introducing you to the world of apps.

Apps provide you with functionality of all kinds, from an app that turns your Kindle Fire into a star-gazing instrument to game apps. You can find calendar apps, drawing apps, and apps that provide maps so that you can find your way in the world.

Exploring the world of apps

You can buy apps for your Kindle Fire by using the Amazon Appstore. This store is full of apps written especially for devices that are based on the Android platform, including Kindle Fire.

Android devices may have slightly different operating systems, and therefore not every app will work on every device. See Chapters 10 and 11 for some suggested apps that will work well with your Kindle Fire.

Follow these steps to explore the world of apps:

1. **Tap the Apps button at the top of the Home screen to enter your Apps library.**

2. **Tap the Store button.**

   The store shown in Figure 4-3 appears.

   At the top of the store is the offer Get a Paid App for Free Every Day.

3. **(Optional) Tap this option to download a free app to your device.**

Figure 4-3:
The Amazon
Appstore.

You can get a different free app every day; just be sure you don't glut your Kindle Fire's memory with free apps you're not really going to use.

Below the free app offer are tabs. The tab labeled Top contains the most popular apps (this tab is active when you first open the store). Additional tabs include

- ✔ **New:** This tab displays the latest apps that have been added to the store.

- ✔ **Games:** Tap this tab to see featured game titles, as shown in Figure 4-4. Across the top of the Games section of the store are tabs such as Action, Adventure, Arcade, Board, Cards, Casino, Casual, Educational, Kids, Multiplayer, Music, Puzzles & Trivia, Racing, Role Playing, and Sports.

Figure 4-4: Games include puzzles, cards, sports, and more.

- ✔ **Entertainment:** Here, you'll find entertainment-related apps such as the IMDb movie database app or Old Time Radio Player. Three tabs — All, Top, and Recommended for You — help you browse for content.

- ✔ **Lifestyle:** This category, shown in Figure 4-5, includes apps for managing various areas of your life, such as home design and relationships. Across the top are tabs including Home & Garden, Self Improvement, Astrology, Relationships, Hair & Beauty, Celebrity, Quizzes & Games, Advice, and Parenting.

✔ **News & Weather:** Tap this tab to see apps that help you keep on top of the latest news and weather information. Across the top are tabs including World, U.S. Newspapers, Business, Politics, Entertainment, Sports, Science & Tech, Health, and Weather.

✔ **Utilities:** These apps help you maintain your Kindle Fire and organize your life. Across the top are tabs including Battery Savers, Alarms & Clocks, Calculators, Calendars, and Notes.

✔ **Social Networking:** Use this tab to find social networking apps for services such as Facebook and LinkedIn.

On the bar containing categories, you are able to view only the beginning of the News & Weather category. Press your finger on the farthest right of this category bar and swipe to the left to reveal the last few categories listed above.

Figure 4-5:
Improve
everything
from your
love life and
garden to
your parent-
ing skills
with these
apps.

You can also tap the Top tab to see the best-selling apps in each category, tap the All Categories tab to view all apps, or tap the Recommended for You tab to see recommendations in that category based on your buying history.

Searching for apps

You can have fun browsing through categories of apps, but if you know which app you want to buy, using the search feature can take you right to it.

To search for an app, follow these steps:

1. **Tap in the Search field.**

   The keyboard shown in Figure 4-6 appears.

Figure 4-6:
Use the search field and onscreen keyboard in the Appstore to find what you want.

2. **Using the onscreen keyboard, enter the name of an app, such as the game Angry Birds Rio.**

   Suggestions appear beneath the Search field.

3. **Tap a suggestion to display the list of suggestions with more detailed results, as shown in Figure 4-7.**

4. **Tap an app name to see more details about it.**

   The Product Info screen appears, as shown in Figure 4-8. Read the description or tap the Photos, Reviews, or Recommendations tabs across the top of the screen to find out more about the app.

TIP

The Save button adds the app to your Saved for Later list. You access this list by tapping the Menu button on the Options bar, tapping More, and then tapping Saved for Later. You can go to this list at any time to buy an item or delete it from the list by pressing and holding your finger on it and then tapping Remove in the menu that appears.

Figure 4-7:
Search
results
in the
Appstore.

Figure 4-8:
Product
details are
shown in
the Product
Info screen.

Buying apps

You might find something you want to own by browsing or searching, but however you find it, when you're ready to buy, you can follow these steps:

1. **From the product description, tap the Price button.**

   Note that if the app is free, this button reads Free, but if you have to pay for the app, the app price (such as $0.99) is displayed on the button. When you tap the button, its label changes to Buy App (for paid apps) or Get App (for free apps). See Figure 4-9.

Figure 4-9:
Tap Buy
App or Get
App to make
the app
your own.

2. **Tap the button again to purchase paid apps and download paid or free apps to your Kindle Fire.**

   A Downloading button appears, showing the download progress. When the installation is complete, an Open button appears.

3. **If you want to use the app immediately, tap the Open button.**

To use the app at any time, locate it in the App library or, if you've used it recently, on the Carousel; tap the app to open it. Each app has its own controls and settings, so look for a settings menu like the one for the Angry Birds Rio game, shown in Figure 4-10.

If you find an app that you like in the store, you can share it with others by using IM or e-mail. Tap the Share button on the app description page in the Amazon Appstore, shown in Figure 4-8, to use this feature.

You can also buy apps from the Appstore on your PC or Mac. When placing the app in your shopping cart, be sure to select Kindle Fire for the device you want to download the app to in the drop-down list below the Add to Cart button. When you complete your purchase, the app is immediately downloaded to your Kindle Fire.

To delete an installed app from your App library, press and hold it until a menu appears. Tap Remove from Device. The app isn't gone. It's still stored in the Cloud, and you can download it again at any time by tapping it in the Cloud tab of the App library.

Settings

Buying Content

Apps are great, but shopping for content is my favorite thing to do. I'm not putting down games and calculators, but to me, content means a night at the movies, a rainy afternoon with a good book, or a relaxing hour listening to a soothing collection of music.

From Amazon, you can buy publications, books, music, and video (movies and TV shows) to download or stream to your Kindle Fire. The buying process is somewhat similar for the different types of content, but there are slight variations, which I go into in the following sections.

Buying publications through Newsstand

There's a world of periodicals out there, from magazines to newspapers, just waiting for you to explore them. Kindle Fire's color display makes browsing through color magazines especially appealing.

If you tap Newsstand on the Home page of Kindle Fire, and then tap the Store button, you see several categories of items (see Figure 4-11).

First, there are Free Trials displayed across the top. You can swipe right to left to scroll horizontally through these.

Figure 4-11:
The
Newsstand
Store.

Below Free Trials, you see categories such as Featured Magazines, Featured Newspapers, and Fashion & Entertainment (though the categories might change on a regular basis).

You can tap the See All button above any category to see a more complete list of included items.

When you find the publication you want, follow these steps to buy or subscribe to it:

1. **Tap the item.**

   A screen appears showing pricing, a description of the publication, and Subscribe Now and Buy Current Issue buttons (see Figure 4-12).

2. **Tap Subscribe Now or Buy Current Issue.**

   The button label changes to read Downloading. When the download is complete, the button label changes to Read Now.

3. **Tap the Read Now button to open the magazine.**

   Note that the magazine is stored in your Amazon Cloud library, where you can read or download it to your Kindle Fire at a later time.

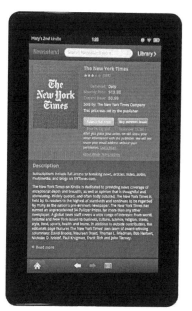

Figure 4-12:
Details
about a
publication
and buttons
to help you
purchase or
subscribe.

Buying books

I may be partial to books because I write them, but I hardly think I'm alone. If you've joined the electronic book revolution (or even if you haven't), you'll find that reading books on Kindle Fire is convenient and economical (e-books are typically a few dollars less than the print version, and you can borrow e-books from your local library for free).

To browse through e-books from Amazon on your Kindle Fire, follow these steps:

1. **Tap the Books button on the Kindle Fire Home screen.**

2. **Tap the Store button.**

   The Amazon Bookstore sports a Recommended for You section at the top, recommending books based on your buying history.

3. **Swipe right to left to scroll horizontally through the recommendations at the top.**

   You also see categories such as Top 100 Paid, Top 100 Free, and New & Noteworthy.

As with the Newsstand, when you locate and tap an item in the bookstore, you see a screen with that item's pricing and description (see Figure 4-13). In the bookstore, the buttons you see at this point are labeled Try a Sample and Buy (or Buy for Free). Here's how these two buttons work:

✔ **Try A Sample:** Tap this button, and it changes to a Downloading button, and then to a Read Sample Now button. Tap the Read Sample Now button to open the sample of the book.

✔ **Buy or Buy for Free:** Tap this button, and it changes to a Downloading button. When the download is complete, the button label changes to Read Now. Tap the Read Now button to open the book. Remember that the book is now stored in your Books library, where you can tap it to open and read it at your leisure.

After you've read a bit of your new book, it will appear both in your Books library and on the Carousel on the Home screen.

To remove a book from your device (remembering that it will still be stored in the Amazon Cloud), open your Book library, press and hold the book, and tap Remove from Device from the menu that appears.

For more about reading e-books and periodicals on Kindle Fire, see Chapter 6.

Figure 4-13:
Details
about a
book in the
Amazon
Bookstore.

Buying music

You may hate computer games, you might not read books very often, but I've never met anybody who doesn't like some kind of music. No matter what kind of music you prefer, from hip-hop to Broadway, you're likely to find a great many selections tucked away in Amazon's vaults.

Tap the Music button on the Kindle Fire Home screen and then tap the Store button. At the top of the Store screen, you see the following tabs: Featured, Bestsellers, New Releases, and Genres. Tap one of these tabs to get a list of items in that category (see Figure 4-14). You can also tap the Albums or Songs tabs to view music by these criteria.

Below these tabs on the Music Store home page, you'll see thumbnails of music selections.

Figure 4-14:
The Amazon
Music
Store.

Follow these steps to buy music:

1. Tap an item.

A screen appears, displaying a list of the songs in the case of an album with Price buttons for both the entire album and each individual song.

2. **Tap the arrow button to the left of a song to play a preview of it.**

3. **Tap a Price button.**

   The button label changes from the price of the item to the word Buy.

4. **Tap the Buy button.**

   The song or album downloads to your Music library. A confirmation dialog box opens, displaying a Go to Your Library button and a Continue Shopping button (see Figure 4-15).

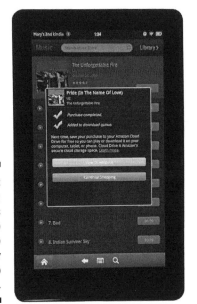

Figure 4-15:
This dialog box allows you to return to your library or keep shopping.

5. **Tap the Go to Your Library button to open the album and display the list of songs.**

   The album is now stored both in your Music library and the Cloud; if you tap on a song to play it, it'll also appear with recently accessed content in the Carousel.

   If you tap the Continue Shopping button, you can later find the album in your Music library.

See Chapter 7 for more about playing music.

Buying video

You should definitely check out the experience of consuming your video programs on a portable device such as Kindle Fire. From lying in bed or on the beach to watching your videos while waiting in line at the bank, portability can be a very convenient feature.

When you tap Video on the Kindle Fire Home screen, you're instantly taken to the Amazon Video Store shown in Figure 4-16.

Figure 4-16:
Shop for video in the Amazon Video Store.

Across the top of the screen, you see thumbnails of items in the Prime Instant Videos category. Beneath these thumbnails is a horizontally scrolling list of thumbnails for movies from $2.99. Beneath this list are thumbnails of items in the category of TV Shows from $1.99.

Tap an item, and a descriptive screen appears. For TV shows, this screen includes episode prices and a set of Season tabs. For movies, this screen offers Watch Trailer, Purchase Options, and 48 Hour Rental buttons (see Figure 4-17).

Tap an episode Price button or a movie Purchase Options button, and the button becomes a Watch Now button. Tap the Watch Now button, and the TV show or movie starts to play.

Figure 4-17:
The video
screen
offers
several
options.

Tap the 48 Hour Rental button for movies, and you see a Rent button. Tap this, and you're immediately charged for the rental. The 48-hour rental period begins when you start to watch the movie.

See Chapter 8 for more about playing videos.

Shopping for Anything Else

Amazon kindly pre-installed an Amazon Shopping app on your Kindle Fire so that you can quickly go to their online store and buy anything your heart desires.

The Amazon Shopping app (see Figure 4-18) is included in your Favorites right out of the box. Just tap it, and Amazon opens in your browser with a list of recommendations for you, based on previous purchases. You can tap the Shop All Departments tab to access a drop-down list of available departments.

Now, just proceed to shop as you usually do on Amazon, tapping any item of interest to add it to your cart and using your Amazon account information to pay and arrange for shipping.

Figure 4-18:
Tap the
Amazon
app to go
shopping
for virtually
anything.

Chapter 5

Going Online

. . . .

. . . .

*Y*ears ago, the best way to stay in touch with the outside world was by reading the morning paper and going to the mailbox to get your mail. Today, browsing the web and checking e-mail has replaced this routine in many of our lives. Kindle Fire can become your new go-to device for keeping informed and in touch by using Amazon's Silk browser and the pre-installed e-mail client.

In this chapter, you discover the ins and outs of browsing with Silk and the simple tools you can use to send and receive e-mail on Kindle Fire.

Getting Online by Using Wi-Fi

Kindle Fire is a Wi-Fi device, meaning that you have to have access to a nearby Wi-Fi network to go online. You might access a Wi-Fi connection through your home network, at work, or via a public hotspot, such as an Internet cafe or airport.

When you first set up your Kindle Fire (as described in Chapter 2), you can choose a Wi-Fi network to use for going online. If you want to log on to a different network, follow these steps:

1. **Tap Quick Settings to open a menu of common settings, such as Volume, Wi-Fi, and Brightness.**

2. **Tap Wi-Fi.**

   Wi-Fi settings appear (see Figure 5-1).

3. **Tap a network in the list of available wireless networks to sign in.**

   You have to enter a password to sign in to some networks.

Figure 5-1:
Use Wi-Fi
settings to
select a
network to
join.

Browsing with Silk

Silk is a brand new browser from Amazon. Some people wondered why Amazon didn't choose to use an existing browser, such as Opera, for Kindle Fire. The answer is that Silk takes advantage of Amazon's ability to use its own servers to make your browsing experience fast.

For example, if you visit a popular news website and choose to tap the headline story to get more details, the odds are many thousands of people have done the same thing. The Silk browser recognizes this pattern and holds that next page in its cache (a dedicated block of memory) to deliver it quickly to you if you also make this selection. This ability makes your browsing experience fast and smooth as, well, silk.

In the following sections, I introduce you to Silk's browser environment. Many tools and features will be familiar to you from other browsers, but a few are unique to Silk.

Using navigation tools to get around

Tap on the Web button at the far right of the library tools displayed across the top of the Kindle Fire Home screen to see Silk, as shown in Figure 5-2.

Address/Search field

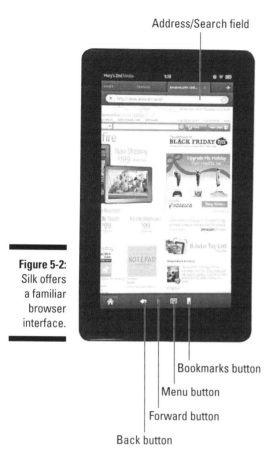

Bookmarks button

Menu button

Forward button

Back button

Figure 5-2:
Silk offers
a familiar
browser
interface.

You can use the Back and Forward buttons to move among pages you've previously viewed. To go directly to a page, tap in the Address field (note that this field will act as a Search field if you enter a word or phrase or as an Address field if you enter a website's address, or URL). Enter a site address and tap Go. The website is displayed.

Silk uses tabs that allow you to display more than one web page at a time and move among those pages. Tap the Add Tab button — which features a plus sign (+) — to add a tab in the browser. When you do, thumbnails of recently visited sites appear. You can tap on a thumbnail to go to that site, or you can tap in the Address bar and enter a URL by using the onscreen keyboard that appears.

Bookmarking sites

You can bookmark sites in Silk so that you can easily jump back to those sites again. With a site displayed on screen, tap the Menu icon in the Options bar and tap Add Bookmark. In the Add Bookmark dialog box that appears (see Figure 5-3), tap OK to bookmark the currently displayed page. You can then tap the Bookmarks button shown in Figure 5-2 to display thumbnails of all bookmarked pages. Tap on one to go there.

Figure 5-3:
Bookmarks
help you
quickly
return to
a favorite
page.

Add bookmark

Name

uters, Books, DVDs & more

Location

http://www.amazon.com/

OK   Cancel

To delete a bookmark, after tapping the Bookmarks button to display thumbnails of bookmarked pages, press and hold a page. In the menu that appears, tap Delete. In the confirming dialog box that appears, tap OK and the bookmark is removed.

When a website is open in Silk, the Menu button on the Options bar also provides a Share Page feature. When you tap this option, you can select to share the current page via Facebook or send a link to a page by using Amazon Email.

Searching for content on a page

Web pages can contain a lot of content, so it's not always easy to find the article or discussion you want to view on a particular topic. Most browsers provide a feature to search for content on a web page, and Silk is no exception.

To search the currently displayed page by using Silk, follow these steps:

1. **Tap Menu on the Options bar.**

2. **On the screen that appears (see Figure 5-4), tap Find in Page.**

   The onscreen keyboard appears with the Search field active.

3. **Type a search term.**

   It appears in an orange box hovering above the first instance of the word on the page. Other instances of the word on that page are highlighted by a white bubble outlined in orange, as shown in Figure 5-5.

4. **Tap any of these bubbles to view the related content.**

5. **Tap Done to end the search.**

Figure 5-4:
Search the
currently
displayed
page.

First instance of word.

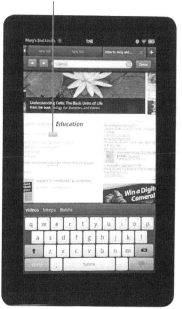

Figure 5-5:
The first
instance of
a word on
a page is
indicated by
an orange
box.

Searching the web

Most of us spend a lot of our time online browsing around to find what we want. Search engines make our lives easier because they help us narrow down what we're looking for by using specific search terms; they then troll the web to find matches for those terms from a variety of sources.

To search the entire web, follow these steps:

1. **Tap the plus sign (+) to add a tab in the browser if you want search results to appear on a new tab.**

   Thumbnails of recently visited sites appear.

2. **Tap in the Search field.**

   The thumbnails change to a list of bookmarked sites, and the onscreen keyboard appears.

3. **Enter a Search term and tap Go.**

   Search results appear in Google (see Figure 5-6).

4. **Tap a result to go to that page.**

To specify a search engine to use other than the default, Google, tap the Menu button in the Options bar, and then tap Settings. Use the Set Search Engine option to choose Google, Bing, or Yahoo! as the default search engine.

Figure 5-6: Search results are displayed in the default search engine you specify — in this case, Google.

Reviewing browsing history

We've all experienced this: You know you visited a site in the last day or so that had a great deal, product, news story, or whatever — but you just can't remember the URL of the site. That's where the ability to review your browsing history comes in handy. Using this feature, you can scan the sites you visited recently organized by day and, more often than not, spot the place you want to revisit.

With Silk open, tap the Menu button on the Options bar. Tap History, and sites you've visited on the Kindle Fire appear in a list divided into categories such as Today and Last 7 Days (see Figure 5-7). Look over these sites and, when you find the one you want, tap it to go there.

Figure 5-7:
To help you find what you want, sites are divided chrono-logically.

To avoid losing a site you know you want to revisit, bookmark it using the procedure in the earlier section, "Bookmarking sites."

Working with web page content

There are a few things you can do to work with contents of websites using Kindle Fire. For example, you may find online content that you want to download, such as a PDF file that you download to your Docs library or an image you download to the photo Gallery. You can also open or share content you find online.

Here's how these work:

- ✔ **View downloads.** Tap Menu on the Options bar, and then tap the Downloads button to view completed downloads.

- ✔ **Save or view images.** Press and hold an image, and a menu appears offering the option to Save Image or View Image (see Figure 5-8).

- ✔ **Open, save, or share links.** Press and hold your finger on any linked text until a menu appears offering these options: Open, Open in New Tab, Bookmark Link, Save Link, Copy Link URL, and Share Link.

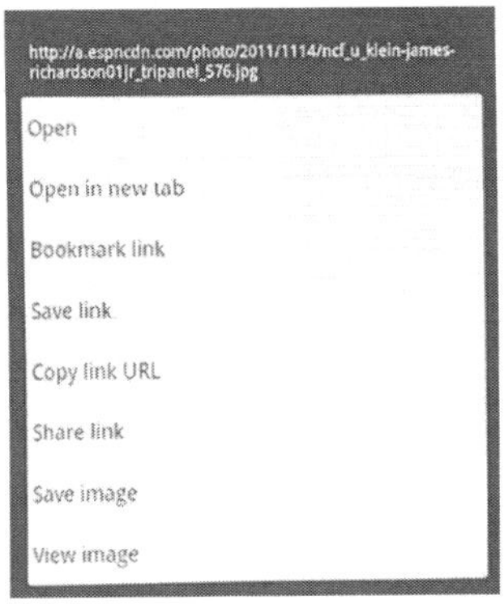

Figure 5-8:
You can work with links and images on your Kindle Fire by using this menu.

http://a.espncdn.com/photo/2011/1114/ncf_u_klein-james-richardson01jr_tripanel_576.jpg

Open

Open in new tab

Bookmark link

Save link

Copy link URL

Share link

Save image

View image

Personalizing Silk

Silk sports a nice, clean interface. Still, there are a few things you can do to personalize the way Silk looks and acts that might work better for you.

With Silk open, tap the Menu button on the Options bar, and then tap Settings. In the screen that appears (see Figure 5-9), here are some of the things you can control about the Silk interface:

- ✔ **Text Size:** To make text on the page more readable, you might want to change the default size of text. Tap Text Size, and then choose Tiny, Small, Normal, Large, or Huge from the menu that appears. (Figure 5-10 shows the Huge setting selected.)

- ✔ **Default Zoom:** Specify Silk's default size of the view as Far, Medium, or Close.

You can also double-tap a page to enlarge the view and double-tap again to reduce the view. Or with your fingers pinched together on the screen, spread them out to enlarge the view. Start with your fingers spread apart and then pinch them together to reduce the view size.

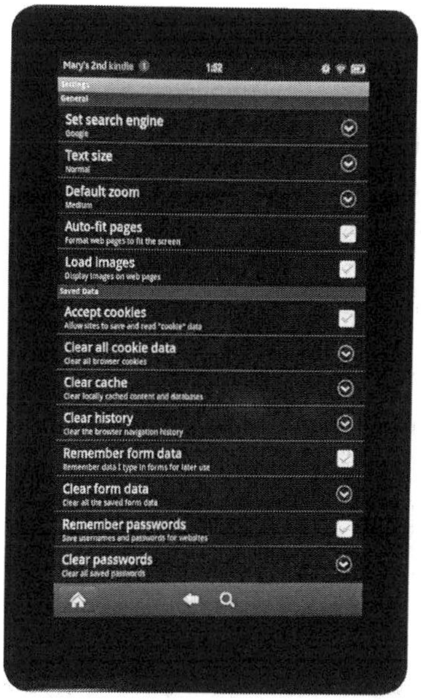

Figure 5-9:
The various
settings
for the Silk
browser.

Figure 5-10:
Huge text
can help
those with
vision
challenges.

✔ **Auto-Fit Pages:** Formats web pages to automatically fit the screen.

✔ **Load Images:** Allows images on web pages to be displayed in the browser.

✔ **Open in Background:** Select this checkbox to open new tabs behind the current tab, rather than in front of it.

If you want to get rid of all the personalized settings you've made to Silk, with Silk open, on the Options bar, tap the Menu button and then Settings. Scroll down to Advanced Settings, and then tap Reset to Default.

Making Privacy Settings

Browsing out there on the Internet can be a bit dangerous. There are people and businesses who want to leave small files on your computer called *cookies* that they use to track your activities or gain illegal access to your online accounts.

Some uses of cookies are perfectly legitimate and allow a reputable business such as Amazon to greet you with personalized recommendations based on your past activities when you visit their sites. Less reputable sites sell your information to others or advertise based on your online history by displaying irritating pop-up windows.

The Privacy settings for Silk help you to stay safe when you're browsing online. Tap the More button on the Options bar, and then tap Settings to view and modify the following privacy settings (see Figure 5-11):

Saved Data	
Accept cookies Allow sites to save and read "cookie" data	☑
Clear all cookie data Clear all browser cookies	⌄
Clear cache Clear locally cached content and databases	⌄
Clear history Clear the browser navigation history	⌄
Remember form data Remember data I type in forms for later use	☑
Clear form data Clear all the saved form data	⌄
Remember passwords Save usernames and passwords for websites	☑
Clear passwords Clear all saved passwords	⌄

Figure 5-11: Privacy settings can protect your personal information as you browse.

✔ **Accept Cookies.** Tap this checkbox to stop sites from downloading cookies to your Kindle Fire.

✔ **Clear All Cookie Data.** You can tap this setting, and then in the Clear dialog box that appears, tap OK to clear all cookies from your device.

✔ **Clear Cache.** Any computing device holds information in its cache to help it redisplay a page you've visited recently, for example. To clear out that cache, which can also free up some memory on your Kindle Fire, tap OK.

✔ **Clear History.** Your Silk browser retains a history of your browsing activity to make it easy for you to revisit a site. However, it's possible for others who view your browsing history to draw conclusions about your online habits. To clear your history, tap OK in this setting.

✔ **Remember Form Data.** If you want Silk to remember data you've entered into forms before — such as your name, mailing address, or e-mail address — to help you complete online fields more quickly, tap this checkbox. The danger here, and the reason you might choose to deselect this checkbox, is that if somebody gets a hold of your Kindle Fire, they could use this feature to gain access to some of your personal information or use your online accounts.

✔ **Clear Form Data.** Clears out any form data you've already saved.

✔ **Remember Passwords.** If you want Silk to remember passwords that you enter for various accounts, tap this checkbox. Just be aware that this setting puts your accounts at risk should you ever misplace your Kindle Fire. One option, if you use this setting, is to require a password to unlock your Kindle Fire Home screen. This setting, which can help protect all content stored on the device, is discussed in Chapter 3.

✔ **Clear Passwords.** If you previously allowed Silk to remember passwords but have a change of heart, you can tap OK in this setting to remove saved passwords.

✔ **Show Security Warnings.** This is a handy feature that requires Silk to check for problems with a website you're trying to visit and warn you of any problems with the site. Tap the checkbox to activate the warnings.

✔ **Enable Plug-ins.** Tap this checkbox to allow plug-ins to run. *Plug-ins* are small programs that enable functionality in a web browser, such as displaying certain types of content.

✔ **Enable JavaScript.** JavaScript is used to run some scripts on web pages, but it has some rather legendary security gaps. Some people prefer not to enable JavaScript when they browse for this reason.

✔ **Block Pop-up Windows.** Tapping this setting opens a dialog box that offers the settings Ask, Never, and Always. You can choose to have Silk ask you whether it should open pop-up windows, never allow pop-ups at all, or always allow pop-ups by tapping the relevant setting.

Working with E-Mail

Kindle Fire has a built-in e-mail client. A *client* essentially allows you to access e-mail accounts you've set up through various providers, such as Gmail and Windows Live Hotmail. You can then open the inboxes of these accounts and read, reply to, and forward messages by using your Kindle Fire. You can also create and send new messages, and even include attachments.

In the following sections, I provide information about setting up and using your e-mail accounts on Kindle Fire.

Setting up an e-mail account

Setting up your e-mail on Kindle Fire involves providing information about one or more e-mail accounts that you've already established with a provider such as Gmail.

Follow these steps to set up an e-mail account the first time you use the app:

1. **Tap Apps.**

   The Apps library appears.

2. **Tap Email.**

   The Email app opens and displays a Start button the first time you open the app.

3. **Tap the Start button.**

   A list of account types appears.

4. **Tap Gmail, Yahoo, Hotmail, AOL, or Other.**

   The dialog box shown in Figure 5-12 appears.

5. **Enter your username and password in the appropriate fields, and then tap Next.**

   A new screen appears, displaying two fields.

6. **Enter the name that will appear on outgoing messages in the Display Name field and a name in the Account Name field to identify the account for yourself.**

   The Account Name is optional.

7. **Tap the Send Mail from This Account by Default check box if you want to set this up as your default e-mail account.**

8. **Tap the View your Inbox button to go to the inbox for the account you just set up.**

Figure 5-12:
The screen
for setting
up your
e-mail
account

You can set up as many e-mail accounts as you like. When you open the
Kindle Fire Email app, you see a Unified Inbox that combines messages from
all accounts you set up, as well as individual inboxes for each account (see
Figure 5-13).

Figure 5-13:
Your Kindle
Fire e-mail
client
inboxes.

To delete an account in the Email app, tap the Menu button in the Options bar
and then tap Accounts. Press and hold your finger on an account; from the
menu that appears, tap Remove Account.

Sending e-mail

After you set up your e-mail account(s), as described in the preceding section, you're able to send e-mails from your Kindle Fire. To create and send an e-mail from the open Email app, follow these steps:

1. **Tap the Compose icon.**

   This icon is the symbol of a small box and pencil at the bottom of the screen, to the left of the Search button.

   A blank e-mail form appears, as shown in Figure 5-14.

Figure 5-14:
A blank form waiting for you to enter an e-mail address, subject, and message.

2. **In the To: field, enter a name.**

   Alternatively, tap the Add Contacts button, which features a plus sign (+), to open the Contacts app and tap on a name there to add that person as an addressee.

3. **If you want to send a copy of the e-mail to somebody, tap the Cc/Bcc button to make those fields appear; then enter addresses or choose them from the Contacts app by tapping the Add Contacts button.**

4. Tap in the Subject field and enter a subject by using the onscreen keyboard.

5. Tap in the Message text field and enter a message.

6. (Optional) If you want to add an attachment to an e-mail, tap the Attach button shown at the bottom of the screen and, in the menu that appears, choose to attach an item from the photo Gallery or the Doc library.

7. To send your message, tap the Send button at the bottom of the screen.

   If you decide you're not ready to send the message quite yet, you also have the option of tapping the Save Draft button and sending it later by tapping the Menu button on the Option bar from your Inbox, tapping Folders, and then opening the Drafts folder.

Here are a couple of handy shortcuts for entering text in your e-mail: The Auto Complete feature lists possible word matches as you type; tap one to complete a word. In addition, you can double-tap to place a period and space at the end of a sentence.

Receiving e-mail

Kindle Fire can receive your e-mail messages whenever you're connected to a Wi-Fi network.

When an e-mail is delivered to your inbox (see Figure 5-15), simply tap to open it. Read it and contemplate whether you want to save it or delete it (or forward or reply to it, as covered in the following section). If you don't need to keep the message, you can delete it by tapping the Trash button in the Options bar.

Forwarding and replying to e-mail

When you receive an e-mail, you can choose to reply to the sender, reply to the sender and anybody else who was included as an addressee on the original message, or forward the e-mail to another person.

If you reply to all recipients, you send an answer to the sender, anybody else in the To: field of the original message, and anybody in the Cc: and Bcc: fields. Because Bcc: fields aren't visible to you as a recipient, you may be sending your reply to people you're not aware of.

Figure 5-15:
Your inbox.

To forward or reply to an e-mail, with the Email app inbox displayed, follow these steps:

1. **Tap an e-mail to open it.**
2. **Tap the Reply button.**

   A menu of options appears.
3. **Tap Reply, Reply All, or Forward (see Figure 5-16).**
4. **If you're forwarding the message, enter a new recipient.**

   If you're replying, the message is already addressed, but you can enter additional recipients if you want to.
5. **Tap in the message area and enter your message.**
6. **Tap the Send button to send your message on its way.**

Organizing your inbox

There are a few methods you can use to keep your inbox organized so that you can find what you need:

Figure 5-16:
Choose to reply to a message or send it on to somebody` else.

- Sort your inbox to see messages by different criteria, such as by sender or by subject. By default, your inbox lists your received messages from newest to oldest. Tap the Newest button in your inbox and choose from the following sort criteria: Oldest, Subject, Sender, Flagged, Read, Unread, Attachments.

- Move messages from one folder to another. Tap the Options bar, and then tap the Menu icon. Tap Folders to view all folders. Next, tap to open a folder and then tap Edit List; all messages are displayed with checkboxes to the left of each (see Figure 5-17). Tap to select a message or messages, and then tap Move at the bottom of the screen. Choose the folder into which you want to move the message from the list that appears, and then tap Done when finished.

- Mark messages you've read as unread to remind you to read them again or delete messages you no longer need by using the Edit List feature.

- Flag messages that are of particular importance. To flag messages, tap the little flag below the time of receipt listed to the right of the message in the Edit List screen.

You can easily search your inbox. Tap the Search button at the bottom of the e-mail screen. Enter a search term in the Search field, and then tap Search on the onscreen keyboard. You can search by sender name, a word in an e-mail, or the e-mail subject.

Figure 5-17:
You can
select mes-
sages to
move, mark
as unread,
or delete
from this
screen.

Sending E-Mail to Your Kindle Account

When you register your Kindle Fire, you get an associated e-mail account, which essentially allows you or others to e-mail documents in Word, PDF, RTF, or HTML format to your Kindle Fire.

The address of the account is displayed in the Docs library. Tap the Docs Library button on the Home screen, and you see a line that reads Send Documents to *YourE-MailAccount*@kindle.com where *Your E-Mail Account* is the name of your Kindle e-mail account.

You or others can e-mail documents to this address, and those documents automatically appear in your Docs library. Note that you might need to go to Amazon by using a browser and change the approved e-mail accounts. Click on Your Account and then on Manage Your Kindle. Click the Personal Document Settings and make sure the account is listed under Send to Kindle Email Settings as approved.

Chapter 6

E-Reader Extraordinaire

Kindle Fire comes from a family of e-readers, so it's only natural that the e-reader you use to read books and magazines on the device is a very robust feature. With its bright, colorful screen, Kindle Fire broadens your reading experience beyond black and white books to color publications such as magazines or graphic novels. Its easy-to-use controls help you navigate publications, bookmark and highlight text, and search your libraries of print content.

In this chapter, you can discover what's available, how you open publications, and how to read and then delete them from Kindle Fire when you're done.

So Many Things to Read!

Amazon started as an online book retailer, although through the years, it has branched out to become the largest retailer of just about everything on the planet. Kindle Fire makes it easy for you to buy your content from Amazon. Although you can buy and sideload content from other sources to Kindle Fire, buying from Amazon ensures that you're dealing with a reputable company and receiving safe content (uncontaminated by malware).

The content you buy from Amazon is automatically downloaded to your Kindle device, which means that not only buying from Amazon's bookstore is easy, but you can take advantage of their vast selection of books. In addition, you can borrow Kindle versions of books from many public libraries.

Amazon has also made deals to make many of your favorite magazines and newspapers available. With magazines and newspapers, you can buy the current issue or subscribe to get multiple issues sent to your Kindle Fire as they become available.

To buy books or magazines for your Kindle Fire, on the Home screen, tap either the Books or Newsstand button, which takes you to your Books or Magazine library.

Tap the Store button; this takes you to the Amazon Kindle bookstore, shown in Figure 6-1. See Chapter 4 for more about how to search for and buy content.

Figure 6-1:
Buy magazines by the issue or subscribe by using Newsstand.

You can also buy content at the Amazon website from your computer and have it download to your Kindle Fire. Just select what device you want it delivered to from the drop-down list below the Add to Cart button before you buy Kindle content.

Amazon uses a technology called Whispersync to download books and magazines to your devices. Kindle Fire uses a Wi-Fi connection, so you need to be connected to a Wi-Fi hotspot to download publications.

Reading Books

After you own some Kindle books, you can begin to read by using the simple e-reader tools in the Kindle e-reader app. You may have used this app on another device, such as your computer, smartphone, or tablet, though each version of this app has slightly different features. In the following sections, I go over the basics of how the Kindle e-reader app works on Kindle Fire.

You can get to the Home screen from anywhere in the e-reader app. If a Home button isn't visible, just tap the bottom of the page to display the Options bar which includes a Home button and a set of tools for navigating a book.

Going to the (Books) library

When you tap Books on your Kindle Fire screen, you open the Books library, containing downloaded content on the Device tab and content in the Cloud on the Cloud tab (see Figure 6-2). The active tab is the one displaying orange text. There's also a Store button you use to go to Amazon's website and shop for books.

Cloud tab   Store button

Device tab

Figure 6-2:
The Books
library
displays all
your book
purchases
on two tabs.

There are also several features in your Books library that you can use to get different perspectives on its contents:

- ✔ **Grid and List views.** Tap Menu on the Options bar to display the Grid View and List View options. These provide views of your books by using large thumbnails on a bookshelf (Grid view, shown in Figure 6-3) or in a text list including title and author, along with an accompanying small thumbnail.

- ✔ **Sort titles.** Use the By Author, By Recent, and By Title buttons to view books by any of these three criteria.

- ✔ **Identify new titles.** If you've just downloaded but haven't started reading a book, there will be a bright yellow banner in the corner of the thumbnail with the word New in it (see Figure 6-4).

Tap the Search button on the Options bar to search your Books library contents by title or author.

Figure 6-3: The Grid view in the Book library.

Opening a book

Ah, the pleasure to be had in opening up a new book, awaiting the adventures or knowledge it has to impart with anticipation! Opening your first e-book is likely to bring you a similar sort of pleasure.

New titles

Figure 6-4:
New titles
are easily
identifiable.

To open a book from the Home screen, tap Books to open the Books library. Locate the book you want to read (swipe upward if you need to reveal more books in the list) and simply tap it. If the book has not been downloaded to your Kindle Fire, it begins to download and takes only seconds to complete.

If you've never begun to read the book, it opens on its title page. If you've read part of the book, it opens automatically to the last page you read. This last read page is bookmarked in the Cloud by Amazon when you stop reading, so no matter what device you use to read it — your Kindle Fire, computer, or smartphone, for example — you go to the last read page immediately.

You can also open a publication from Favorites or the Carousel. Read more about these features in Chapter 2.

Navigating a book

An open book just begs to be read. You're used to flipping pages in a physical book, but an e-reader provides you with several ways to move around it.

The simplest way to move one page forward or one page back is to tap your finger anywhere on the right or left side of the page, respectively. Try this to move from the title page to a page of text within the book. With a book page displayed, tap it to see the tools shown in Figure 6-5, including a button to take you to the Kindle Fire Home screen, a Back button to go back one screen, a Font menu to make adjustments to the appearance of fonts and the page, a Menu button to access additional settings, and a Search button to initiate a search for text in the book.

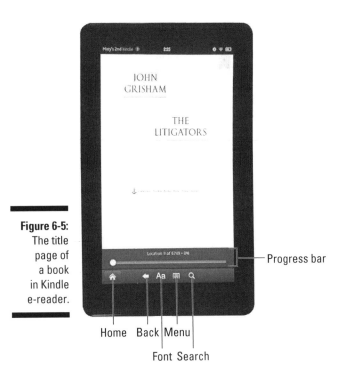

Figure 6-5:
The title
page of
a book
in Kindle
e-reader.

Progress bar

Home Back Menu

Font Search

You can also tap the Menu icon in the Options bar and choose from these options to move around your book:

- **Cover:** Display the book cover.
- **Table of Contents:** Go to the table of contents, if there's a table of contents available for the current title; some children's books and novels, for example, have no table of contents.

✔ **Beginning:** Return to the beginning of the book.

✔ **Location:** Display the dialog box shown in Figure 6-6. Location is calculated by the number of bits of information in the book up to the current location. You can note the location of a particular page by checking this information above the progress bar at the bottom of any page. Tap in the location field and use the onscreen keyboard to enter that location, and then tap OK to go there.

Figure 6-6:
Enter a
location in
the book to
jump there
instantly.

✔ **Sync to Furthest Page:** This option moves you to the last page you read in the book by using any Kindle reader apps or devices.

✔ **My Notes & Marks:** Opens a list showing the location of bookmarks, highlights, and notes that you've inserted into the book (see more about how to do this in the section "Bookmarking and highlighting," later in this chapter), as shown in Figure 6-7. Tap a selection to go that page.

The progress bar along the bottom of the screen indicates how far along in the publication you are at the moment. To move around the publication, you can press the circle on this bar and drag it in either direction.

Figure 6-7:
A list of your
bookmarks,
highlights,
and notes.

Reading children's books

Many children's books with extensive illustrations use what Amazon refers to as a *fixed layout,* meaning that the pages are fixed representations of how the pages look in the print book. This means that you can't enlarge and reduce the size of everything on the page at one time, you can't change the font style, and you can't change orientation: Each book is set in either landscape or portrait orientation. To move from page to page, you can swipe from right to left on the right page to flip it over.

Keep in mind that children's books are usually set up with blocks of text that go along with illustrations; that's why you can't enlarge text on an entire page; instead, you enlarge a single block of text. To do this, double-tap a block of text, and the text becomes larger. When you subsequently swipe the page, you move to the next block of text, which enlarges (the previous block of text goes back to normal size). When you've read the last block of text on the page (typically in a two-page spread), swiping takes you to the next page. Double-tap the currently enlarged text again to go back to normal text size and proceed through the book.

Although the Option bar choices and Progress bar are the same as in other books, pressing the Font button in a children's book results in the message Font Style Options Are Not Available for This Title.

Searching in a book

Want to find that earlier reference to a character so that you can keep up with a plot? Or do you want to find any mention of Einstein in an e-encyclopedia? To find words or phrases in a book, you can use the Search feature.

Follow these steps to search a book:

1. **With a book open, tap the page to display the Option bar, if necessary.**

2. **Tap the Search button in the Option bar.**

   The Search dialog box and onscreen keyboard are displayed, as shown in Figure 6-8.

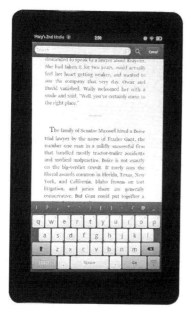

Figure 6-8: Search for a word or phrase by using this Search dialog box.

3. **Enter a search term or phrase, and then tap the Search key on the keyboard.**

   Search results are displayed, as shown in Figure 6-9.

Figure 6-9:
Search
results
indicate
the search
term with a
highlight.

If you'd rather search the web, press a word or phrase to highlight it, and then in the resulting dialog box, tap the More button. At this point, you can tap either Search in Book, Search Wikipedia, or Search Google. The Google option takes you to search results for the term in the Google search engine, and the Wikipedia option takes you to the entry in the popular online encyclopedia that matches your search term. Tap the Back button when you want to return to the e-reader app.

Bookmarking and highlighting

If you find that perfect quote or a word you just have to read again at a later time, you can use the Highlight or Bookmark feature in Kindle e-reader.

To place a bookmark on a page, display the page and tap it to reveal the Bookmark button (a plus sign in the top-right corner of the page), and then tap the button. A small bookmark ribbon appears on the page (see Figure 6-10).

To highlight text, press and hold your finger on the text. Small handles appear on either side, as shown in Figure 6-11. If you want to select additional adjacent text to be highlighted, press your finger on one of these triangular handles and drag to the left or right. When the entire phrase or paragraph you want to highlight is selected, press the selected text to display a menu, and then tap Highlight.

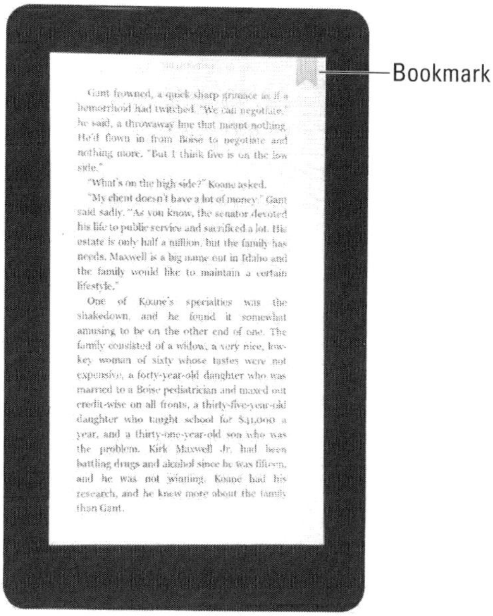

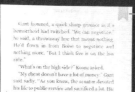

Bookmark

Figure 6-10:
A book-
marked
page.

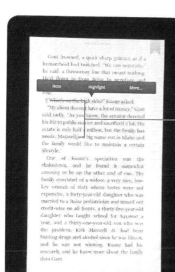

Handles

Figure 6-11:
Click either
handle to
enlarge
the area of
selected
text.

When you place a bookmark on a page or highlight text within a book, you can then display a list of bookmarks and highlights by tapping the Menu button in the Option bar and choosing My Notes & Marks (see Figure 6-12). You can jump to the page indicated by a bookmark or to highlighted text by tapping an item in this list.

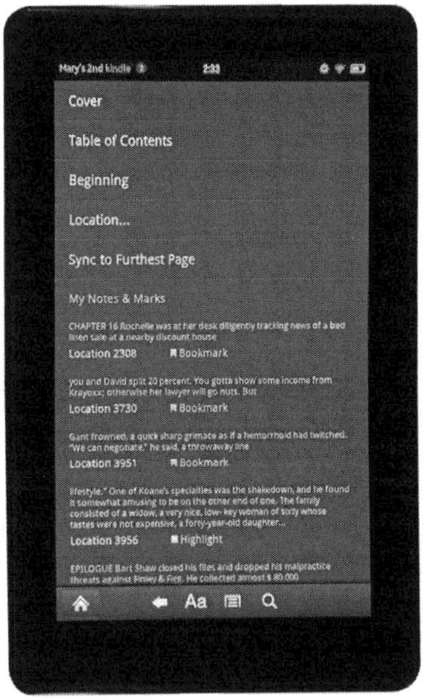

Figure 6-12:
Both high-
lights and
bookmarks
are listed.

When you press text and see the menu shown in Figure 6-11, a brief definition appears from the pre-installed New American Oxford Dictionary. In the definition window, tap Full Definition to go to the full Oxford dictionary definition. Tap the Back button to return to the book. See Chapter 9 for more about Kindle Fire's built-in dictionary.

Modifying the appearance of a page

There are several things you can do to control how things appear on a page in Kindle e-reader. First, you can make text larger or smaller. Second, you can adjust the width of margins. You can also modify spacing between lines. Finally, you can choose a white, black, or sepia-toned background for a page.

To control all these settings, tap the page to display the Options bar, and then tap the Font button (the one with a capital and lowercase A). The options shown in Figure 6-13 appear:

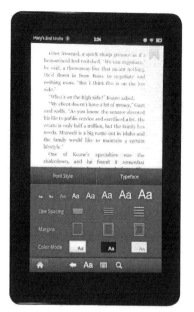

Figure 6-13:
Font options
offer you
some con-
trol over the
appearance
of your
pages.

✔ **Font Size:** Tap a particular font sample to change the size.

✔ **Line Spacing:** Choose how much space to put between lines.

✔ **Margins:** Choose the margin setting you prefer.

✔ **Color Mode (black on white, white on black, black on sepia):** Tap a setting to display a different color page background. A sepia background may make reading easier on your eyes, for example.

You can adjust brightness manually or have Kindle Fire do it automatically. Tap the Quick Settings button at the top-right corner of the screen, and then tap the Brightness button. If you turn Automatic Brightness on, the Kindle Fire will adjust brightness of the screen to compensate for ambient light conditions. If you turn Automatic Brightness off, you can use the slider to adjust brightness. Press the circle on the slider and move it to the left or right to adjust brightness.

Managing publications

After you purchase content on Amazon, from apps to music and books, it's archived in your Amazon Cloud library. If you finish reading a book on Kindle Fire, you can remove it from your device. The book is still in the Amazon Cloud, and you can re-download it to your Kindle Fire at any time.

To remove a book or magazine from your Book library, follow these steps:

1. **Tap Books or Newsstand to display your library.**

2. **Locate and press your finger on the item.**

   A menu appears (see Figure 6-14).

3. **Tap Remove from Device.**

The thumbnail of the item remains in your Books library on the Cloud tab and on the Carousel or Favorites if you've placed it there. To download and read the book again, just double-tap it in any of these locations, and the download begins.

Unlike video and music, which you can stream from the Cloud without ever downloading them, books, magazines, and newspapers can't be read from the Cloud, they must be downloaded to a Kindle device before you can read them.

The Keep or Don't Keep option in the menu in Figure 6-14 relates to the issues of periodicals. At some point, old issues will be removed from your device unless you choose to keep them by using this command.

Figure 6-14:
Use this
menu to
remove a
publication
from Kindle
Fire.

Book samples will offer only a Delete option when you get to Step 3 above. The pre-installed New Oxford American Dictionary offers only the option of adding it to Favorites.

Reading Periodicals

Reading magazines and newspapers on your Kindle Fire is similar to reading books, with a few important differences. You navigate magazines a bit differently and can display them in two different views.

Follow these steps to read a magazine or newspaper:

1. **From the Home screen, tap Newsstand.**

2. **Tap a magazine or newspaper in the Newsstand to read it.**

   Alternatively, you can tap an item on the Carousel from the Home screen.

   If the publication hasn't been downloaded to the device, it begins to download now.

   With the Options bar visible, thumbnails of all pages in the publication are displayed along the bottom of the screen (see Figure 6-15).

3. **Swipe right or left to scroll through these pages, or drag the scroll bar indicator left or right.**

Figure 6-15:
Scroll through thumbnails of pages to find the one you want.

4. **When you find the page you want, tap that page to display it full screen.**

   The Menu button on the Options bar displays contents of the current issue.

5. **Tap an item in the table of contents to go to that item.**

Reading docs on Kindle Fire

Reading docs on your Kindle Fire is a much more straightforward proposition than reading e-books (meaning there are fewer things you can do to navigate around a doc or format the appearance of text). Tap the Docs button on the Home screen, and then locate and tap a document; or tap a doc on the Carousel or Favorites sections of the Home screen to open it.

Swipe left or right to move from page to page or use the slider along the bottom to move around the document.

Pinch and unpinch your fingers on the screen to enlarge and reduce the size of the view.

In Word docs, you can make notes and highlights, but not in PDF documents. To do this in a Word doc, press a word to display a menu, and then tap Note or Highlight in that menu. You can read more about docs and Kindle Fire in Chapter 9.

As with books, you can double-tap to enlarge text on the page; double-tap again to reduce the size of the text. You can also pinch and unpinch the touchscreen to move between larger and smaller views of a page's contents.

Some periodicals can appear in two views:

- **Text view:** In Text view, you see articles in more of an e-reader format (meaning that you get larger text with no columns and no images). In Text view, there's a Font button on the Options bar offering Font Style and Typeface tabs to adjust the size and font used for text. There's also a Style choice for changing Size, Spacing, Margins, and Color Mode (page background).

- **Page view:** Page view shows an exact image of the publication's pages, with all columns and photos intact. You can scroll through the magazine, view it in landscape or portrait orientation, and pinch and unpinch to zoom in and out of the pages.

Tap the Page View or Text View button in the top-right corner of a displayed periodical to switch between these views (if the periodical offers this feature).

Chapter 7

Playing Music

Music has become ubiquitous in most of our lives. Portable devices provide us with decent-quality sound systems for listening to everything from Lady Gaga to Mozart, everywhere from the subway to the jogging path.

The ability to tap into Amazon's tremendous Music Store and sideload music from other sources by using a micro-B cable means that you can build up your ideal Music library and take it with you wherever you go.

In this chapter, you learn about getting music onto your Kindle Fire (see Chapter 4 for more about shopping for music) and how to use the simple tools in the library to play your music and create playlists.

Exploring the Music Library

All your music is stored in the Music library (see Figure 7-1), which you display by tapping the Music button on the Kindle Fire Home screen. The currently playing or last played song and playback controls are located at the bottom of the screen.

Figure 7-1:
The Music
library is
your cen-
tral music
repository.

Currently playing selection

The library is organized by Playlists, Artists, Albums, and Songs, as shown in
Figure 7-2. Tap on any of these tabs to display the associated content.

Figure 7-2:
The Artists
tab shows
available
content by
performer.

At the bottom of the screen, in the Options bar, is a Back arrow to move you
back one screen in the library, the Menu icon, and a Search icon to help you
find pieces of music.

If you tap the Menu button, you see four additional options:

- ✔ **Downloads:** Tap Downloads to see items in the process of downloading, as well as completed downloads.
- ✔ **Settings:** See the sidebar "Music library settings," in this chapter, for details.
- ✔ **Clear Queue or Now Playing:** This setting will change depending on whether you're displaying the currently playing music. From the list of songs in an album, tap Now Playing to display the currently playing music full screen with music playback controls (see Figure 7-3). If you are displaying the full screen of the currently playing music, tap the Clear Queue command to stop the music and go back to the Music library home screen.
- ✔ **Help:** Tap Help to get more information about using the Music app.

TIP

When you tap the Search button on the Options bar, you bring up a search field. Tap in the field and enter the title of a piece of music or a performer, and then tap Search on the onscreen keyboard. Kindle Fire displays results on each of the tabs in the Music library that match the search term(s).

Figure 7-3:
Currently
playing
music.

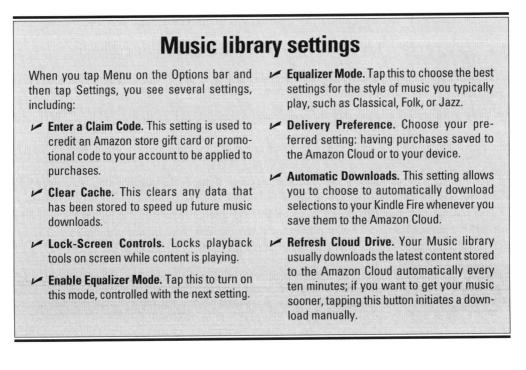

Music library settings

When you tap Menu on the Options bar and then tap Settings, you see several settings, including:

✔ **Enter a Claim Code.** This setting is used to credit an Amazon store gift card or promotional code to your account to be applied to purchases.

✔ **Clear Cache.** This clears any data that has been stored to speed up future music downloads.

✔ **Lock-Screen Controls.** Locks playback tools on screen while content is playing.

✔ **Enable Equalizer Mode.** Tap this to turn on this mode, controlled with the next setting.

✔ **Equalizer Mode.** Tap this to choose the best settings for the style of music you typically play, such as Classical, Folk, or Jazz.

✔ **Delivery Preference.** Choose your preferred setting: having purchases saved to the Amazon Cloud or to your device.

✔ **Automatic Downloads.** This setting allows you to choose to automatically download selections to your Kindle Fire whenever you save them to the Amazon Cloud.

✔ **Refresh Cloud Drive.** Your Music library usually downloads the latest content stored to the Amazon Cloud automatically every ten minutes; if you want to get your music sooner, tapping this button initiates a download manually.

Uploading Music to the Cloud

One way to add music to your Kindle Fire Music library is by buying it from the Amazon Music Store.

You can also transfer a musical selection or collection stored on your computer (the music you've bought through iTunes, for example) by using a micro-B cable connection. (Read more about this process in Chapter 4.)

In addition, the Amazon Cloud allows you to upload music from your computer; after you upload music, it's available to you through your Kindle Fire Music library.

Follow these steps to upload music to the Amazon Cloud:

1. **Go to** `www.amazon.com/cloudplayer` **on your PC or Mac.**

2. **Sign into your Amazon account.**

   The page shown in Figure 7-4 is displayed.

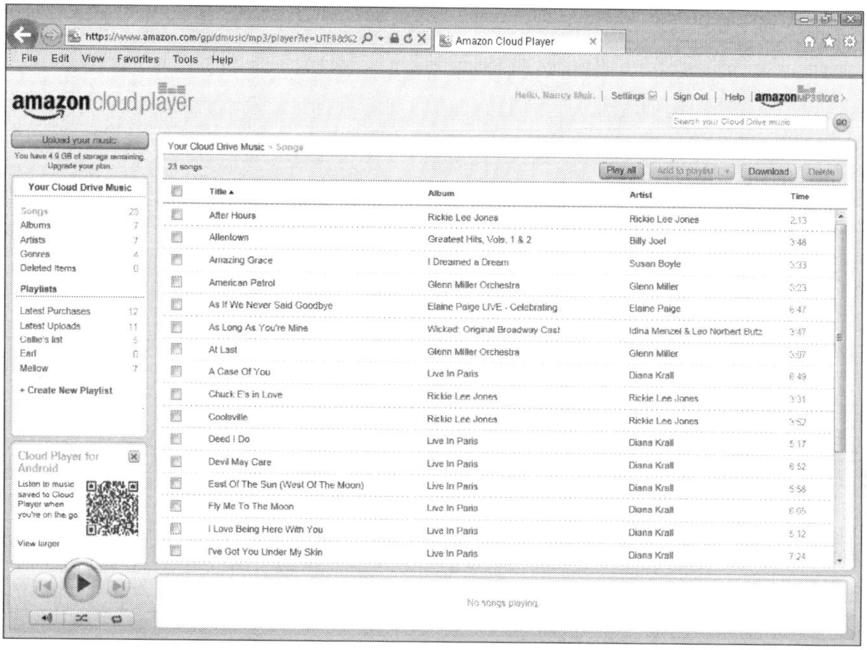

Figure 7-4:
The Amazon
Cloud Player
is where
all your
Amazon-
purchased
music
resides.

3. **Tap the Upload Your Music button.**

   A dialog box appears, asking you to get the Amazon MP3 Uploader.

4. **Tap Download Now and follow the instructions that appear to install the Uploader.**

   After the Uploader has been installed, you see the Upload Music to Your Cloud Library dialog box shown in Figure 7-5.

5. **Tap the plus sign (+) to expand your musical selections on your computer and choose individual items.**

   Alternatively, don't choose anything at this point to upload all music from your computer to the Amazon Cloud.

6. **Tap the Start Upload button.**

   The dialog box shows the upload progress and lists the remaining items to be uploaded. Note that there's also an estimated time to upload the content shown in the dialog box.

After you upload items to your Amazon Cloud library, they are available to Kindle Fire on the Cloud tab of the Music library (see Figure 7-6).

Figure 7-5:
Tap into all
your music
by using the
Uploader.

Figure 7-6:
Music
stored in
the Amazon
Cloud Player
listed in
your Kindle
Fire library.

Playing Music

After you have some music available to play (which I explain how to do in the preceding sections), playing that music is an easy task, one that will make fine use of your experience with every other music player you've ever encountered.

Opening and playing a song

First, you have to locate an item to play, and then you can use the playback toolbar to control the playback. Follow these steps to play music from your Music library:

1. **Tap the Music button on the Kindle Fire Home screen.**

2. **Locate an item you want to play on a tab in the Music library, such as Songs or Artists.**

3. **If you open a tab other than Songs, you need to tap to open an album or playlist to view the contents.**

4. **Tap to play it.**

   If you tap the first song in a group of music selections, such as an album or playlist, Kindle Fire begins to play all selections, starting with the one you tapped.

5. **Use the controls shown in Figure 7-7 to control playback.**

Tap the button with horizontal lines in the top-right of the screen to go back to the album or playlist the song belongs to. Then, to return to the Now Playing screen for the song (see Figure 7-8), tap the song's image at the top-right corner of the album or playlist screen.

You can adjust playback volume by tapping Quick Settings and then Volume, or use the Volume setting in the Now Playing controls.

If you want to use a headphone with your Kindle Fire, which can improve the sound and remove extraneous noise, plug a compatible headphone into the headphone jack at the bottom of the device, near the Power button.

Figure 7-7:
Most of
these
tools are
standard
playback
tools you've
probably
seen before.

Back | Forward
Shuffle Pause/Play Restart

Speaker icon

Figure 7-8:
The
currently
playing song
sports a
little orange
speaker in
this list.

Creating playlists

Playlists allow you to create collections of songs that transcend the boundaries of albums or artists. For example, you might want to create a playlist for a romantic evening, a dance party, or a mellow road trip.

When you tap Music on the Home screen, you see the Playlists tab. Tap it, and you see two default playlists, Latest Purchases and Latest Uploads (see Figure 7-9). There's also a Create New Playlist button.

Figure 7-9:
The items you buy and download are stored in playlists.

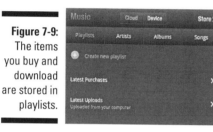

To create a new playlist, follow these steps:

1. **Connect to a Wi-Fi network if you aren't already connected.**

   Creating a playlist requires a Wi-Fi connection because playlists are saved to the Cloud.

2. **Tap Create New Playlist.**

3. **In the screen that appears (see Figure 7-10), enter a playlist name and tap Save.**

   Kindle Fire displays a screen containing a Search field and a list of songs stored on the device.

4. **Tap the Add Song (+) button to the right of any song to select it.**

   If you've stored a lot of music and want to find a song without scrolling down the list, enter a song name in the Search field till the list narrows down to display it.

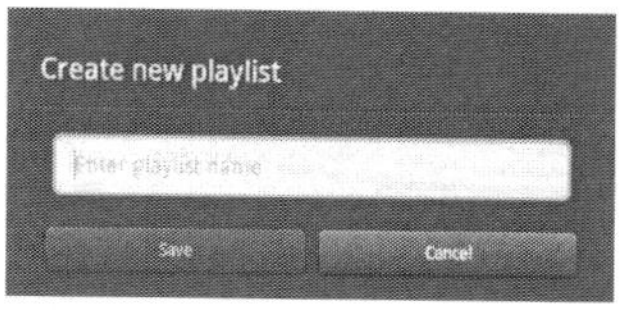

Figure 7-10:
Assign a descriptive name for your playlist.

Create new playlist

Enter playlist name

Save   Cancel

5. **Tap Done to save your playlist.**

The Playlist is displayed (see Figure 7-11) and includes an Edit button that you can tap to edit the playlist contents.

Edit button

Figure 7-11:
A saved
playlist.

You can play the newly created playlist by simply tapping the Playlist tab and then tapping the list you want to play.

When you tap the Edit button on a playlist, you see an Add button and a Done button in the Edit screen. Songs appear with a Delete (–) symbol next to them; tap this symbol to delete a song. Tap Add (+) to choose more songs to add to the playlist. Finally, tap Done when you're done editing.

Chapter 8

Playing Video

Playing video, both movies and TV shows, is a great use of Kindle Fire. The device has a bright, crisp screen, can easily be held in one hand, and is capable of streaming video from the Amazon Cloud, making a typically seamless viewing experience without hogging memory on the tablet itself.

In addition, Amazon offers an amazing selection of video content, including absolutely free Prime Instant Videos (as long as you maintain a Prime account with Amazon).

You can discover the ins and outs of buying video content in Chapter 4. In this chapter, I explain how Amazon streams video content from the Cloud to your device, give you a look at the Kindle Fire Video library, and cover the steps involved in playing a video.

Streaming versus Downloading

When you tap the Video button on the Kindle Fire Home screen, you're immediately taken to the Amazon Video Store (see Figure 8-1), rather than to a library of video titles. That makes sense because, by design, Kindle Fire is best used to stream videos from the Cloud. The device's relatively small memory (8GB) can't accommodate a large number of video files, so instead, Amazon makes it easy for you to stream video to the device without ever downloading it. To go to your Video library, tap the Library button in the top-right corner.

Video content might include Prime Instant Videos (see Figure 8-2), a feature which offers thousands of titles for free with an Amazon Prime account. (You get one free month of Amazon Prime with your Kindle Fire, after which you can purchase a membership for $79 a year.) You can also purchase or rent other video programs and stream them from the Cloud.

Figure 8-1:
The Amazon Video Store offers thousands of titles.

Figure 8-2:
Browse thousands of free titles in the Prime Instant Videos selection on Amazon.

Amazon's Whispersync technology keeps track of the spot in a video where you stopped watching. You can later resume watching that video at that exact location on Kindle Fire, a PC or Mac, or one of over 300 compatible TVs, Blu-ray Disc players, or other devices.

You *can* download videos you purchase (you can't download Prime Instant Videos, however), which is useful if you want to watch them away from a Wi-Fi connection. It's a good idea to remove them from the device when you're done to save space. To delete a video from your device, open the Video library and tap the Device tab. Press and hold your finger on the video, and then tap Remove from Device in the menu that appears.

Looking at Your Video Library

I'm betting a lot of you are going to find that viewing video on your Kindle Fire is a great way to get your entertainment. The Kindle Fire Video library may become your favorite destination for buying, viewing, and organizing your video content.

When you tap Video on your Kindle Fire Home screen, the Amazon Video Store opens (refer to Figure 8-1).

The Store shows three video categories: Prime Instant Videos, Movies, and TV Shows. Tap any category name to see items in that category. When you display a category, on the screen that appears (see Figure 8-3), there are Movies, Prime, All, and TV tabs that you can use to go to other categories.

Tap the View All button in the Store to show all items organized by popularity.

Tap the Library button to go to your Video library (see Figure 8-4). The library sports two tabs — one lists all your videos stored in the Cloud, and one includes videos you've purchased that have been downloaded to the device. The tab that has orange lettering is the active tab.

In addition to the Cloud and Device tabs, there are tabs for filtering content by Movies or TV programs. Note that there's no search function you can use to find the content you're looking for.

Figure 8-3:
A category
of videos in
the Video
Store.

Figure 8-4:
The Kindle
Fire Video
library.

Downloaded video content is listed chronologically by the date you down-loaded it.

Tap the Menu button on the Options bar to display two items — Settings and Help. In Settings (see Figure 8-5), you can view the Device ID and access the Disable HD Purchase Warning setting. If you disable this feature, it turns off a warning that tells you that, although you can play high-definition videos on Kindle Fire, they won't play in high definition because it's not a high-definition device.

Figure 8-5:
You'll prob-
ably want
to disable
this warning
after seeing
it once or
twice.

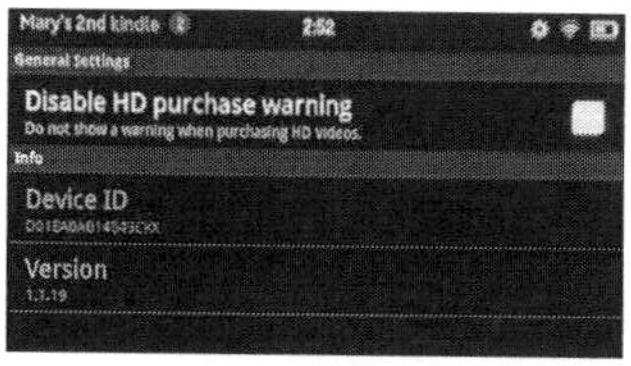

You can also use the By Recent and By Name buttons to view your video content by one of these sort criteria.

Opening and Playing a Video

Playing a video is a simple process. If the video has been downloaded to your device, open the library (tap Video, and then tap the Library button), locate the video (using methods described in the preceding section), and then tap the video to play it.

If you're streaming a video you've purchased from the Cloud, follow these steps:

1. **Tap the Cloud tab.**

   Videos you've rented (whose rental period hasn't expired) or purchased are displayed.

2. **Double-tap an item to open it.**

   If it's a TV show, you see episodes listed (see Figure 8-6); tap one to open it. If it's a movie, at this point, you see a description of the movie.

3. **Tap the Watch Now button.**

   The playback controls appear.

4. **If you've already watched part of the video, tap the Resume button (see Figure 8-7).**

   If you'd rather see the video from its start, tap the Play from Beginning button.

The movie appears full screen (see Figure 8-8). The title of the Movie appears at the top of the screen.

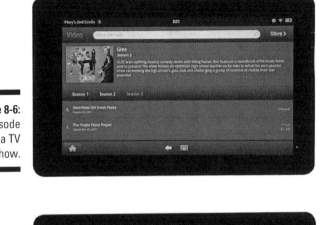

Figure 8-6:
The episode list for a TV show.

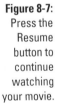

Figure 8-7:
Press the Resume button to continue watching your movie.

Note that the Kindle Fire screen provides an extra-wide viewing angle. This means that you and those watching with you can see the content from the side as well as from straight on.

The familiar playback tools available here include

✔ Play

✔ Pause

✔ A progress bar

✔ A volume slider

✔ A button that moves you ten seconds back in the video

There's also a Back button in the Options bar that you can tap to stop play-back and return to the Kindle Fire Video library. The More Episodes button goes back to all episodes of a TV show.

When you display a video's details in the Amazon Video Store, you can tap the Rental & Purchase Details link to view the terms of use for playing the video.

10 seconds back   Volume slider

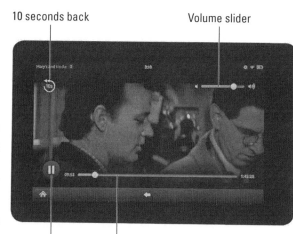

Figure 8-8:
A movie with
playback
controls on
Kindle Fire.

Play/Pause   Progress bar

Chapter 9

Getting Productive with Kindle Fire

Kindle Fire isn't just about watching movies and playing music. There are several ways in which you can use the device to get your work done and share documents and images with others.

In this chapter, I help you explore how Kindle Fire helps you view and share documents. I suggest some ways to make Kindle Fire even more of a productivity tool by investing in a software suite and using the pre-installed Contacts app. Finally, if you need to view or edit photos for work or play, here's where you get to explore what the simple photo app, Gallery, has to offer.

Understanding Kindle Docs

One of the items you see across the top of your Kindle Fire Home screen is the Docs library (see Figure 9-1). Documents will be stored in the Docs library, to which this button provides access, and if you've viewed them recently, they may also be available on the Carousel. You can also save docs to Favorites on the Home screen (see Chapter 2 for more about Favorites).

Figure 9-1:
Tap the
Docs button
to open the
Docs library.

Docs button

In the following sections, you can discover how docs get onto your Kindle Fire and how you can view and share them. I also provide some advice about using productivity software on Kindle Fire to get your work done.

Getting docs onto Kindle Fire

Documents help you communicate information in forms ranging from newsletters to memos and garage sale flyers to meeting agendas.

Documents come in different formats. Some formats come from the originating software, such as Microsoft Word. Other formats can be opened by a variety of software programs, such as RTF documents that can be opened by any word processor program. In Kindle Fire, supported document formats include Microsoft Word, HTML, RTF, or PDF, as well as Amazon's Mobi or ASW formats.

To get a doc onto your Kindle Fire, you can sideload it from your PC or Mac by using the optional Micro-B connector ($10 from Amazon) or e-mail it to yourself at your Kindle e-mail address (locate this address by opening your Docs library; it's listed near the top).

If you send a document to your Kindle e-mail address, the file appears in your Docs library automatically. Kindle formats (.mobi and .azw) are also supported, and some documents will be converted to this format automatically. Kindle Fire even supports compressed (Zip) file formats and automatically unzips them when they're transferred to your device via e-mail.

Although you can view these documents, as shown in Figures 9-2 and 9-3, at this point in time, you can't edit them on your Kindle Fire.

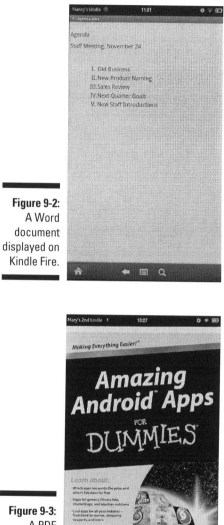

Figure 9-2:
A Word
document
displayed on
Kindle Fire.

Figure 9-3:
A PDF
document
displayed on
Kindle Fire.

To sideload docs to your Kindle Fire, purchase a micro-B cable from Amazon or another source, and then follow these steps:

1. **Attach the micro-B end of the cable to your Kindle Fire (see Figure 9-4).**

2. **Attach the USB end of the cable to your computer.**

   Your Kindle Fire will appear as a drive in Windows Explorer or the Mac Finder.

3. **Click the appropriate choice to open and view files on the drive that appears (see Figure 9-5).**

4. **Click and drag files from your hard drive to the Docs folder in the Kindle Fire window.**

   You can also copy and paste documents from one drive to the other.

5. **Tap the Disconnect button on your Kindle Fire to safely eject the Kindle Fire from your computer.**

You can now unplug the micro-B cord from your Kindle Fire and computer.

 Docs are only stored on your Kindle Fire, not backed up to the Amazon Cloud. If you want to back up documents, use the micro-B cable to copy them back to your computer.

Figure 9-4: A micro-B cable attached to a Kindle Fire.

Figure 9-5:
Your Kindle
Fire appears
like an
external
drive on
your com-
puter when
attached
using a
micro-B
cable.

Opening docs

After you put a doc onto your Kindle Fire by either sideloading it from a computer or receiving it through Kindle e-mail, you can view the document by
following these steps:

1. **Tap the Docs button on the Kindle Fire Home screen to open the Docs
   library.**

   Alternatively, you can locate recently viewed docs on the Carousel and
   docs you've saved to Favorites in the Favorites area of the Home screen.

2. **When the library opens (see Figure 9-6), tap a tab to see the library
   contents.**

   You can choose one of two categories: By Recent or By Title.

3. **When you find the document you want to view, tap to open it.**

Figure 9-6:
The Docs
library, by
Recent or
By Title.

On the Options bar, if you tap the Menu icon, you can select Grid view or List view. Grid view displays items as thumbnails (see Figure 9-7); List view displays items in a textual list with smaller thumbnails alongside.

At this point in time, you can only view documents, and with Word format documents, you can add notes and highlights. However, you can't edit them at all.

Figure 9-7:
The Grid
view of the
Docs library.

E-mailing docs

When you have a doc on your Kindle Fire, you can view it and also share it with others as an e-mail attachment. Follow these steps to attach a doc to an e-mail message:

1. **Tap the Apps button on the Home screen.**

   A list of installed apps appears.

2. **Tap the E-Mail app.**

   The E-Mail app opens.

3. **Tap your Inbox and then tap the compose icon.**

   This is the symbol of a small box and pencil at the bottom of the screen, to the left of the Search button.

   A blank e-mail form appears, as shown in Figure 9-8.

4. **Enter a name in the To: field, a subject, and a message.**

5. **Tap the Attach button, shown at the bottom of the screen in Figure 9-8.**

   In the menu that appears (see Figure 9-9), choose to attach an item from the photo Gallery or Quickoffice. If you choose Quickoffice, you can then tap on the Recent Documents or Internal Storage folders. Internal Storage will include folders for various libraries, including Documents.

6. **Tap Send.**

   Your document goes on its way, attached to your e-mail.

Figure 9-8:
A blank form waiting for you to enter an e-mail address, subject, and message.

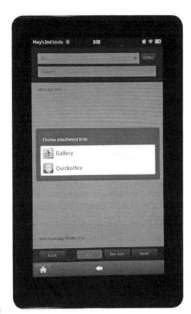

Figure 9-9:
Attaching
a doc to an
e-mail
message.

Taking documents further

If you want to do more than view documents on your Kindle Fire, consider using the built-in app called Quickoffice (see Figure 9-10). Available in free and paid versions (Quickoffice Pro, whose apps are listed in Figure 9-11, will cost you $14.99), this productivity suite for Android smartphones works on Kindle Fire, giving you word processor, spreadsheet, and presentation software.

Another option you can check out is OfficeSuite Pro 5, which lets you view and edit Microsoft Word and Excel documents and view Microsoft PowerPoint files.

Also consider using an online productivity suite such as Google Docs or Office Live. These websites offer hosted software you can use to create and edit documents online. Both are compatible with the Microsoft Office Suite, and you can access them and work with online docs by using the Silk browser. See Chapter 5 for more about Silk.

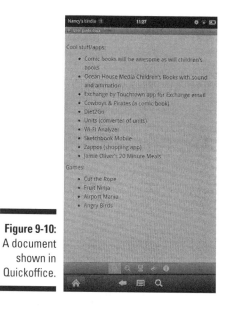

Figure 9-10:
A document
shown in
Quickoffice.

Figure 9-11:
Quickoffice
Pro offers
common
office pro-
ductivity
tools.

See Chapter 10 for a list of great apps you can get to flesh out your Kindle Fire functionality, such as calendar, calculator, and note taking apps.

Managing Contacts

The Contacts app pre-installed on Kindle Fire is a basic but useful contact management tool. You can enter or import contact information, sort that information by several criteria, and use Contacts to address e-mails.

You can find Contacts by tapping the Apps button on the Kindle Fire Home screen. Tap the Contacts app to display its main screen, as shown in Figure 9-12.

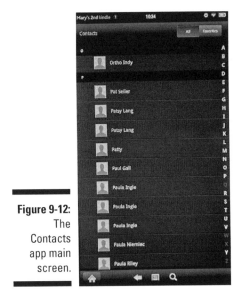

Figure 9-12: The Contacts app main screen.

Creating new contacts

It's data entry time! Before you can use your contacts, you need to get them onto Kindle Fire. The manual way to do that is to simply create new contacts and enter the information in the New Contact form.

To create a new contact, follow these steps:

1. **Tap the Menu button on the Options bar and then tap the New Contact button to create a new contact.**

   The New Contact screen that appears (see Figure 9-13) contains fields including Name Prefix, First Name, Middle Name, Last Name, and Name Suffix.

Figure 9-13: The New Contact screen.

2. **Tap in a field and enter text.**

   The onscreen keyboard appears when you tap in a field.

3. **When you're done entering text in one field, tap the Next button on the onscreen keyboard to go to the next field.**

   Be sure to scroll to the bottom and enter phone and e-mail address information. You can also expand fields for Postal Address and Organization.

4. **Tap the Photo icon to add a photo.**

   The Gallery appears (see Figure 9-14).

5. **Double-tap to open a photo album; then tap a photo to display it.**

   The photo appears full screen.

6. **Move the arrows on the edges of the orange box surrounding the image to crop it, if you want.**

7. **Tap Save.**

   You return to the New Contact form.

8. **Tap the Save Changes button to save the new contact.**

Figure 9-14:
The photo
Gallery may
contain sev-
eral albums.

*Photos used by permission of Ashley
Ernstberger Photography*

Viewing contacts

You can use various settings to control how your contacts are organized and
even save contacts within your Favorites.

To sort your contacts, on the Options bar, tap Settings. There are two
options here for sorting contacts (see Figure 9-15):

✔ **Sort List By:** First Name or Last Name

✔ **View Contact Names As:** First Name First or Last Name First

Tap each setting and choose your sort preference from the list that appears.

You can also choose to view contacts in the Favorites area of the Home
screen. To add a contact to Favorites, follow these steps:

1. **Tap Apps; then tap Contacts to open the Contacts app.**

2. **Tap the All tab.**

3. **Press and hold the contact name with your finger.**

   A star appears next to the contact's name, as shown in Figure 9-16.

4. **In the menu that appears, tap Add to Favorites.**

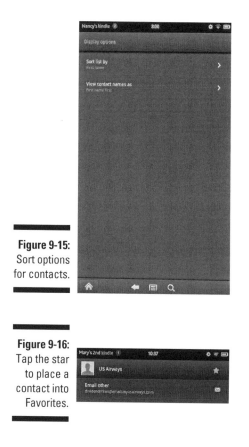

Figure 9-15:
Sort options
for contacts.

Figure 9-16:
Tap the star
to place a
contact into
Favorites.

Viewing Photos

Kindle Fire has a pre-installed photo app for all you photography lovers.
Though its features are pretty basic, Gallery allows you to view and do minor
edits to photos.

Getting photos onto Kindle Fire

The Kindle Fire has no camera, so you have to get photos onto the device
by copying them from your computer by using a micro-B cable (see the section "Getting docs onto Kindle Fire," earlier in this chapter, for more about
this procedure). Using this procedure, you can copy photos into the Pictures
folder on your Kindle Fire by using Windows Explorer or the Mac Finder.

Viewing photos

After you load photos into your Pictures library and disconnect the micro-B cable, you can tap the Apps button on the Kindle Fire Home screen, and then tap Gallery. This displays an album that represents the folder you copied to your Kindle Fire (see Figure 9-17). If you copy another folder of photos, it will come over as a separate album. Photos in albums are organized chronologically by the date you placed them on your Kindle Fire.

Figure 9-17:
Photo
albums in
the Gallery.

Photos used by permission of Ashley
Ernstberger Photography

There are three main actions you can perform to view pictures:

- ✔ Tap to open an album and view the pictures within it.
- ✔ Tap a picture to make it appear full screen.
- ✔ Swipe left or right to move through pictures in an album.

Working with photo tools

When you display a photo enlarged to full screen, the More icon on the Options bar contains the following items:

✔ **Details:** This option shows you the photo's Title, Type (such as JPEG), Created on Date, Album (the Pictures album, by default), and File Size. Tap OK to hide these details.

✔ **Crop:** With a picture enlarged, tap this option to display a cropping square superimposed on the image. Drag the edges of this square to crop to the section of the photo you want to use, and then tap Save (see Figure 9-18).

✔ **Rotate Left:** Tap this tool to rotate the image 180 degrees to the left.

✔ **Rotate Right:** Tap this tool to rotate the image 180 degrees to the right.

Figure 9-18:
Use this cropping tool to remove sections of a picture you'd rather not show.

— Cropping tool

Photo used by permission of Ashley Ernstberger Photography

Note that you can also enlarge or reduce a photo by pinching and unpinching with your fingers on the touchscreen.

When you display a photo full screen, you see tools at bottom of the screen, including Zoom In, Zoom Out, and a tool that causes the image to fit within the screen again if you've enlarged it.

To share a photo with others, tap the Options bar, tap Share, and then tap Send with Email. In the e-mail message that appears with the photo already attached, enter an address, subject, and message, and then tap the Send button.

Using the New American Oxford Dictionary

If you swipe from right to left on your Carousel, you find that the item at the very bottom of your Carousel is the New Oxford American Dictionary. Amazon thoughtfully provided this book to help you find your way with words.

In addition to being able to browse through the dictionary, when you press and hold a word in a book or magazine, a dictionary definition from the New Oxford American Dictionary is displayed. You can tap the Full Definition button to go to the full dictionary entry (see Figure 9-19).

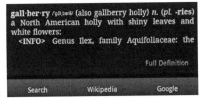

Figure 9-19: A definition displayed in an e-book.

When you open the dictionary, you can flick from page to page; entries are arranged here alphabetically, as with any dictionary. You can also use the Linked Entries links to go to related terms from any definition (see Figure 9-20).

Figure 9-20: Many entries have linked entries that provide related information.

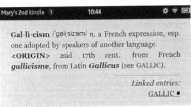

As with any book, you can tap the Font button on the Options bar to adjust font size, line spacing, margins, and the background color of the pages. That's about all there is to the dictionary, but it can prove to be a handy resource for those who love words.

See Chapter 6 for more about reading all kinds of e-books on Kindle Fire.

Keeping your finger on the Pulse

Another neat pre-installed app you can use to enlighten yourself is Pulse, a news aggregator. This app allows you to choose from among various sources of content, such as *The New Yorker* or ESPN Headlines, and then access them from one central location. You can find Pulse already saved to your Favorites when you start Kindle Fire for the first time (the icon for the Pulse app is shown here).

Chapter 10

Ten Apps That Add Functionality to Kindle Fire

*A*ny mobile device today, from a smartphone to a tablet, thrives on the thousands of apps that make a world of features available.

Kindle Fire has functionality built in for consuming books, periodicals, music, and video, as well as a contact management app, web browser, and e-mail client. However, there are some tools that many of us have grown used to having available that you can easily acquire by adding apps to the device.

Amazon Appstore, which you can learn the ins and outs of using in Chapter 4, contains thousands of cool apps for you to explore. To help you flesh out the basic tools in Kindle Fire, in this chapter, I provide reviews of apps such as a calendar, note taker, and unit converter that meet your day-to-day needs and whet your *app*etite. Most of these are free.

From a nutrition guide to a very cool calculator app, these will provide you fun and useful functionality for your Kindle Fire and not cost you much more than the time to download them.

SketchBook Mobile Express

From: AutoDesk, Inc.

Price: Free

SketchBook (see Figure 10-1) is a drawing app to satisfy the creative artist in your soul. With 47 preset brushes, you can draw whatever you can imagine on your Kindle Fire screen. You can control the brush characteristics and make use of an extensive color palette.

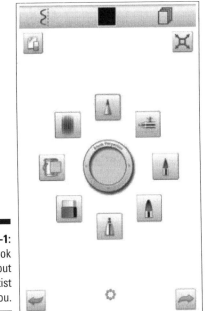

Figure 10-1:
Sketchbook
brings out
the artist
in you.

Try sideloading photos and modifying them with this clever app, then save your files in JPEG, PNG, or PSD formats. When you're done, it's easy to e-mail your artistic efforts to yourself to print from your computer.

The Brush Properties circular control lets you easily adjust the size and opacity of the writing tools. Touch the square at the top of the screen to access color controls and watch the Red, Blue, and Green levels adjust as you move around the color wheel.

However, be careful of the Erase button in the upper-left corner of the screen: I've erased more than one picture by tapping this when I shouldn't have!

Fast Food Nutrition Lite

From: FastFood.com

Price: Free

If you're watching your weight but are forced to scarf down fast food now and then, this little app could have an impact on your waistline. Not limited to traditional drive-thru fast food joints, the app gives you nutritional information about dishes from 100 restaurant chains, such as Applebees, Chili's, and Checker's, and includes over 25,000 menu items (see Figure 10-2).

Fast Food Nutrition Lite helps you keep track of calories, Weight Watchers points, fats, trans fats, saturated fats, cholesterol, sodium, carbohydrates, sugars, and protein. The calorie counter shows you how much of the recommended daily allowance each meal is providing you. Select the items you want in your meal and touch View Order, which displays a handy screen showing you all the totals for your meal.

Figure 10-2: Keep track of your calories with this handy counter.

You can add thumbnails for your favorite restaurants so that you don't have to search through all the restaurants to find the ones you like best.

You sometimes pay a price to get a free app. In the case of this app, and several others, that price is having to view ads as you use the app.

aCalendar

From: Mathias Laabs

Price: Free

Kindle Fire has no built-in calendar app, so this one is a natural to add to your apps collection. This easy-to-use calendar app can help keep you on schedule (see Figure 10-3). You can display day, week, month, and birthday views. For you astronomers out there, you can even check on phases of the moon. The month screen displays black dots for full moons and a half-filled dot to indicate a half moon.

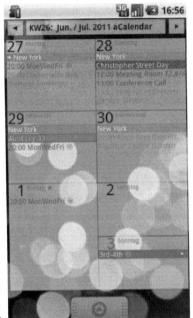

Figure 10-3: Keep track of your week with aCalendar.

aCalendar makes great use of touchscreen gestures to let you easily move among views and take a look at event details. Swipe the screen horizontally to change among day, week, and month views. Swipe vertically to move from day to day, week to week, or month to month. Because the app also takes advantage of the Android native calendar, it uses very little battery power.

You can also add events to your calendar by simply pressing a date and fill-ing in the name and time of your event.

Astral Budget

From: Astral Web, Inc.

Price: Free

If you're like many of us, these days, you're tightening your belt and counting those pennies. Astral Budget is an app that helps you keep track of all your expenses, whether for a single trip or your yearly household budget. You can use built-in categories for fixed spending such as rent, food, travel, utilities, and so on to categorize your expenses.

The app has four sections: Goals, Expenses, Reports, and Export. Using these, you can enter the amounts you want to spend and track them against actual expenditures. You can use the wide variety of Reports in Astral Budget (see Figure 10-4) to examine your spending trends and even export data to your computer to examine with the more-robust application Excel. I like the Chart selections, including bar charts, pie charts, and list charts.

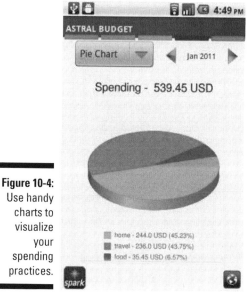

Figure 10-4: Use handy charts to visualize your spending practices.

ColorNote Notepad Notes

From: Social & Mobile, Inc.

Price: Free

Kindle Fire also doesn't include a note-taking app, and if you're like me, you need one. If being able to keep a to-do list warms the cockles of your organized (or disorganized) heart, this is a neat little free app, and it's very simple to use.

You can keep a simple to-do list or other random notes, and even share information with your friends via e-mail, social networks, or messaging (honey, here's the shopping list for your evening commute!).

ColorNote allows some nice word-processing-like functions, such as the ability to edit and cross items off lists that are completed (see Figure 10-5).

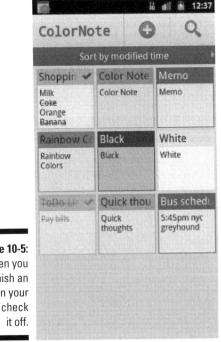

Figure 10-5:
When you finish an item on your list, check it off.

You can even set up reminders for items in your notes and search for specific content.

If your notes are top secret, consider using the password feature in ColorNote.

Cube Calculator

From: IP

Price: Free

It's a good idea to add a calculator to Kindle Fire, if only to figure out tips and your sales commissions, right? This is a calculator with tons of bells and whistles, from the ability to use mathematical expressions and time calculations to logarithmic and trigonometric functions. There's a secondary keyboard for additional functions, such as cosines (see Figure 10-6).

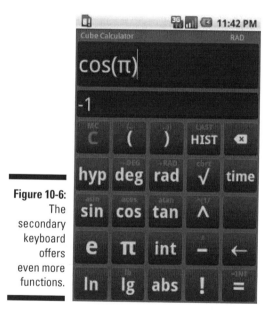

Figure 10-6: The secondary keyboard offers even more functions.

Even if you're not a power math user, the very nice interface in this app makes casual calculations simple to do. Also, the help system for this app is actually helpful.

You can choose a theme such as Light or Dark to ease your eyestrain as you calculate. You can also control the maximum number of digits to be returned in a result (after all, who needs pi to go on ad infinitum?).

Handrite Note

From: Ben Lee

Price: $2.99

If you miss the feeling of writing notes by hand, instead of typing them on plastic keyboards, this app is for you. It's simple to use: Tap to create a new note, and then use the spiral-bound pad interface to write words or draw images on the page with your finger. You can change the stroke width and text size for your writing and even use different colors (see Figure 10-7).

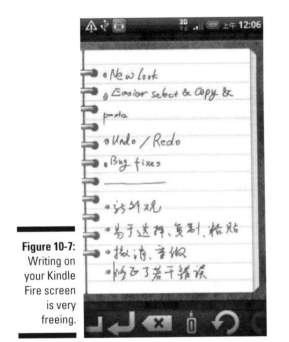

Figure 10-7: Writing on your Kindle Fire screen is very freeing.

When you close the app, your note is saved, but you can press and hold the touchscreen to edit the text you entered. You can also create a label for a note and export it. The app isn't fancy; it's more for jotting down a phone number when you see a flyer about a missing kitten or making a quick note to yourself about what to pick up at the store, but for what it is, it's darn handy and easy to use.

Exchange by TouchDown

From: NitroDesk, Inc.

Price: Free

If you want to access mail, contacts, and calendar information from your workplace and your company uses Microsoft Exchange Server for these accounts, this little app will help you tap into your company e-mail. It touts itself as providing great security and provides the very handy service of wiping data from your Kindle Fire remotely if it's lost or stolen.

Keep in mind that TouchDown doesn't work with IMAP or POP3 servers; it's intended for Exchange Servers, as well as supporting Zimbra, Kerio, and ActiveSync. Though the app has pretty-easy-to-use settings (see Figure 10-8), you might want to sit down over a cup of coffee with your network administrator to get this one working. But when you do, I think you'll be pleased.

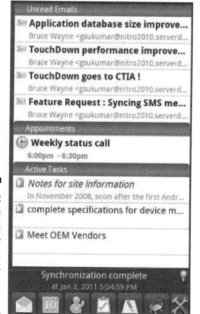

Figure 10-8: Make settings yourself or enlist the aid of your administrator.

Units

From: staticfree.info

Price: Free

If, like me, you need help converting just about anything to anything else (feet to meters, pounds to kilos, or whatever), you'll appreciate this handy little app. It handles 2,400 different conversions, including height, weight, volume, volume to weight, and time to distance. Tap the Unit key, and you'll see a list of the various types of conversions available (see Figure 10-9).

Just fill in the You Have field and the You Want field, and then enter the number of units. Tap the equal sign (=) and get your conversion. Holding Kindle Fire in landscape orientation displays a few more helpful tools on the calculator style interface.

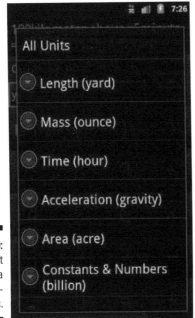

Figure 10-9: Tap the Unit key to get a list of common units.

Wi-Fi Analyzer

From: farproc

Price: Free

Because Kindle Fire can connect to the web only through Wi-Fi, this handy app is helpful for keeping track of local Wi-Fi connections. You can observe available Wi-Fi channels and the signal strength on each (see Figure 10-10). There are several styles of graph to choose from, including Channel, Time, Channel Rating, and Signal Meter.

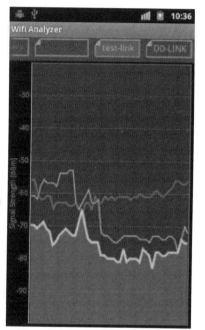

Figure 10-10: Figure out whether your nearest Wi-Fi will help you connect.

Chapter 11

Ten (or So) Top Gaming Apps

*P*eople using tablets will tell you that one of the great uses for them is to play games of all sorts. From card games such as solitaire to graphically entertaining new classics like Angry Birds and Fruit Ninja, having access to games helps you while away a quiet evening at home or keep yourself from getting bored in boring settings, such as the security line at the airport or the dentist's waiting room.

In this chapter, I introduce you to 11 great games that will provide hours of fun and create the core of your Kindle Fire gaming library.

Cut the Rope

From: Zepto Lab

Price: $0.99

This is a very addictive game (ask my husband, I'm a Cut the Rope widow). The whole idea is that there's this monster you have to feed candy (don't ask why). The candy swings on ropes (see Figure 11-1), and you have to figure out how to cut the rope so the candy whacks into various star-shaped objects, exploding them, and eventually ends up in the monster's mouth.

Along the way, you encounter various devices, such as little air blowers that help you manipulate items on the screen and achieve your goals. Of course, you'll want to turn off the annoying music and little sounds that seem to come from the candy. In the Menu setting on the Options bar, tap the little speaker to mute the sound. Then, have fun feeding the monster!

Figure 11-1:
Figure out
which rope
to cut to
whack the
stars and
feed the
monster.

Plants vs. Zombies

From: PopCap Games, Inc.

Price: $2.99

If you're somebody who worries about zombies attacking your home (and who doesn't?), this game will appeal to you. A phalanx of zombies waits on the street outside your house. You get to put plants in your front lawn to spit little seeds to cut down the zombies as they approach. You have to tap small suns that appear to grow new plants that you can then place on your lawn to defeat yet more attacks (see Figure 11-2).

As you proceed through levels of the game, you get additional items, such as sunflowers, walnuts, and berries, that you can use in your attempts to thwart the zombies. At some point, you're told the final wave of zombies is coming; if you survive the next minute or so, the zombies are defeated, and you get a new type of plant or fruit to use in your next defense against them.

Don't ask why. Just try it.

Figure 11-2:
Oh no! Stop those zombies in their tracks!

Fruit Ninja

From: HalfBrick Studios

Price: $0.99

This game combines the concept of a ninja warrior and fresh fruit. Somehow, I believe this makes the mayhem that ensues less violent in nature. Essentially, pieces of fruit are thrown up on the screen, and you use your finger to swipe across them, cutting them in half (see Figure 11-3). The trick is that occasionally a bomb gets thrown up with the fruit and you have to be quick enough to not swipe at the bomb; otherwise, you blow it up and end the game.

Figure 11-3:
Who knew that slicing fruit could be so fun?

If bombs aren't your thing, you can play the Zen mode, where you're merely slicing up fruit with no bombs involved. If you've had a hard day at the office, trust me, this one is great to work out your tensions (just imagine the fruit is, well, anybody or anything that really annoyed you today).

Quell

From: Fallen Tree Games

Price: $0.99

Quell is a peaceful afternoon in the park compared to some of the other games listed here. It doesn't involve bombs or zombies. Instead, you get a playing board with a small raindrop on it. You can move the raindrop up or down a row to collect the pearly objects in its path while peaceful oriental music plays in the background.

The trick is that you have to figure out how to get the raindrop to hit objects not already in its path. Sometimes, you have to shift the raindrop from one side of the board to the other, move up, then over, then down, and so on until you're in line with the object you want to hit (see Figure 11-4).

As you proceed through levels, you get new challenges that require some brain power. But the whole experience is much more relaxing and peaceful than many games you find these days.

Figure 11-4: This little brain teaser will keep your mind sharp.

Airport Mania Free

From: Amazon Digital Services

Price: Free

Imagine you're an air traffic controller. You sit in front of your Kindle Fire screen, allowing incoming planes to land, taxi to the terminal, let passengers off, move to a holding area, and take off again. Sounds easy, right?

It is until you have five or six planes coming in and out. Then, it becomes seriously like rubbing your stomach while patting your head as a tornado approaches (see Figure 11-5). But give it a try. Nothing really crashes and nobody dies, so what can you lose?

One nice option in this game is the ability to turn the annoying music off but leave the cool sound effects on.

Figure 11-5:
This game turns multi-tasking into an art form.

Angry Birds (Ad Free)

From: Rovio

Price: $0.99

For anybody into game apps, Angry Birds is no stranger. But if you've never played this classic game, your time has come. There is some backstory here: The pigs absconded with some baby birds, and now the birds are out for revenge. The game consists of pigs hidden in odd structures and birds that you launch using a slingshot to topple the structure and bump off the pigs (see Figure 11-6).

The beauty of this game is that it really does require some skill to figure out exactly where to hit a structure to make it topple and to determine how to use the different types of birds (from bomb birds to boomerang birds) to best effect.

If you love this game, consider getting Angry Birds Rio, where your targets are monkeys and the setting is the tropics.

Figure 11-6:
A true
classic,
Angry Birds
gets your
aggressions
out!

Chess Free

From: AI Factory

Price: Free

If chess is your thing, you'll enjoy this electronic version. You can play the computer or play against another person using the same Kindle Fire. With the latter approach, the board swaps around after each play so that the next person can take his or her turn. There's a game timer if you're in Chess Tournament mode. You can also change the style of the pieces and board.

Tap a piece, and then the game shows you all possible moves unless you turn off Show Legal and Last Moves in the game's Options. Tap the place on the board where you want to move the piece (see Figure 11-7). If you have a change of heart, this game includes a handy Undo button.

Figure 11-7:
If you love
chess, try
out this
version.

Jewels

From: MH Games

Price: Free

If you have a thing about jewelry, or even if you don't, you might enjoy
Jewels. This matching game lets you play with jewel-colored baubles to
your heart's content. The idea is that you can flip two gems on this grid-like
game board if doing so will allow you to line up three items of the same kind
(see Figure 11-8). When you do, the lines of gems shift to provide a different
arrangement.

There are a few other rules, such as getting more points for chain reactions
and scoring bonus points. The game is over when there are no more possible
three-of-a-kind matches left.

Figure 11-8:
Simple yet colorful, Jewels promises hours of fun.

Wordsmith

From: Second Breakfast Studios

Price: $2.49

Wordsmith is kind of like the popular word game Scrabble. You build words from available tiles and take advantage of double-letter and triple-word tiles (as shown in Figure 11-9) to score extra points.

The game definitely gets you thinking about how to utilize tiles already in place to one-up yourself or your opponent. The game accommodates two to four players. Build up your vocabulary while having fun with Wordsmith.

As with many games, this one comes in a free version, as well. Free versions may include advertisements and offer more limited levels of play.

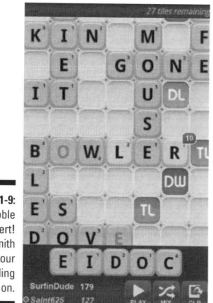

Figure 11-9:
Scrabble
fan alert!
Wordsmith
gets your
spelling
mojo on.

Solitaire Free Pack

From: Tesseract Mobile Software

Price: Free

There aren't too many surprises to this game, but for those who are devoted to solitaire, it offers an electronic version you can play on the go on your Kindle Fire (see Figure 11-10). Rack up the points with 43 different games, including Klondike, Pyramid, and Monte Carlo.

Figure 11-10:
If you're
alone, try
a round of
solitaire.

You can change the card backgrounds and track your game scores to see whether you're improving as you go. If you want to, you can take advantage of the unlimited redo feature to try and try again to win a game.

Random Mahjong

From: Paul Burkey

Price: Free

What I like about this game is that there are no time limits, no super bonus points to earn. You just take your time matching the nicely designed tiles (see Figure 11-11) layer by layer. You can control the look of the game and get hints when your brain is getting tired.

Figure 11-11: This traditional matching game involves more strategy than you think!

You do need to pay attention to how you unearth tiles from lower layers so that you can play them, and you can choose to play on larger and somewhat more complex boards. But other than that, this is a nice way to spend a rainy afternoon with nobody to beat and no exploding elements whatsoever.

And one for the old timers

It's not exactly a game, but for those of you who know who Burns and Allen were, you should definitely check out the very entertaining app Old Time Radio. Download it, and you'll find that it comes with a treasure trove of old-time radio shows — from radio science fiction shows like *Flash Gordon,* to *Mercury Theater, Superman,* and *Jack Benny.* Perhaps a good way to relax between rounds of play of Fruit Ninja and Plants vs. Zombies?

Index

Apple & Macs

iPad For Dummies
978-0-470-58027-1

iPhone For Dummies,
4th Edition
978-0-470-87870-5

MacBook For Dummies, 3rd
Edition
978-0-470-76918-8

Mac OS X Snow Leopard For
Dummies
978-0-470-43543-4

Business

Bookkeeping For Dummies
978-0-7645-9848-7

Job Interviews
For Dummies,
3rd Edition
978-0-470-17748-8

Resumes For Dummies,
5th Edition
978-0-470-08037-5

Starting an
Online Business
For Dummies,
6th Edition
978-0-470-60210-2

Stock Investing
For Dummies,
3rd Edition
978-0-470-40114-9

Successful
Time Management
For Dummies
978-0-470-29034-7

Computer Hardware

BlackBerry
For Dummies,
4th Edition
978-0-470-60700-8

Computers For Seniors
For Dummies,
2nd Edition
978-0-470-53483-0

PCs For Dummies,
Windows
7 Edition
978-0-470-46542-4

Laptops For Dummies,
4th Edition
978-0-470-57829-2

Cooking & Entertaining

Cooking Basics
For Dummies,
3rd Edition
978-0-7645-7206-7

Wine For Dummies,
4th Edition
978-0-470-04579-4

Diet & Nutrition

Dieting For Dummies,
2nd Edition
978-0-7645-4149-0

Nutrition For Dummies,
4th Edition
978-0-471-79868-2

Weight Training
For Dummies,
3rd Edition
978-0-471-76845-6

Digital Photography

Digital SLR Cameras &
Photography For Dummies,
3rd Edition
978-0-470-46606-3

Photoshop Elements 8
For Dummies
978-0-470-52967-6

Gardening

Gardening Basics
For Dummies
978-0-470-03749-2

Organic Gardening
For Dummies,
2nd Edition
978-0-470-43067-5

Green/Sustainable

Raising Chickens
For Dummies
978-0-470-46544-8

Green Cleaning
For Dummies
978-0-470-39106-8

Health

Diabetes For Dummies,
3rd Edition
978-0-470-27086-8

Food Allergies
For Dummies
978-0-470-09584-3

Living Gluten-Free
For Dummies,
2nd Edition
978-0-470-58589-4

Hobbies/General

Chess For Dummies,
2nd Edition
978-0-7645-8404-6

Drawing
Cartoons & Comics
For Dummies
978-0-470-42683-8

Knitting For Dummies,
2nd Edition
978-0-470-28747-7

Organizing
For Dummies
978-0-7645-5300-4

Su Doku For Dummies
978-0-470-01892-7

Home Improvement

Home Maintenance
For Dummies,
2nd Edition
978-0-470-43063-7

Home Theater
For Dummies,
3rd Edition
978-0-470-41189-6

Living the
Country Lifestyle
All-in-One
For Dummies
978-0-470-43061-3

Solar Power Your Home
For Dummies,
2nd Edition
978-0-470-59678-4

Internet

Blogging For Dummies,
3rd Edition
978-0-470-61996-4

eBay For Dummies,
6th Edition
978-0-470-49741-8

Facebook For Dummies,
3rd Edition
978-0-470-87804-0

Web Marketing
For Dummies,
2nd Edition
978-0-470-37181-7

WordPress
For Dummies,
3rd Edition
978-0-470-59274-8

Language & Foreign Language

French For Dummies
978-0-7645-5193-2

Italian Phrases
For Dummies
978-0-7645-7203-6

Spanish For Dummies,
2nd Edition
978-0-470-87855-2

Spanish
For Dummies,
Audio Set
978-0-470-09585-0

Math & Science

Algebra I
For Dummies,
2nd Edition
978-0-470-55964-2

Biology For Dummies,
2nd Edition
978-0-470-59875-7

Calculus For Dummies
978-0-7645-2498-1

Chemistry For Dummies
978-0-7645-5430-8

Microsoft Office

Excel 2010 For Dummies
978-0-470-48953-6

Office 2010 All-in-One
For Dummies
978-0-470-49748-7

Office 2010 For Dummies,
Book + DVD Bundle
978-0-470-62698-6

Word 2010 For Dummies
978-0-470-48772-3

Music

Guitar For Dummies,
2nd Edition
978-0-7645-9904-0

iPod & iTunes For
Dummies, 8th Edition
978-0-470-87871-2

Piano Exercises
For Dummies
978-0-470-38765-8

Parenting & Education

Parenting For Dummies,
2nd Edition
978-0-7645-5418-6

Type 1 Diabetes
For Dummies
978-0-470-17811-9

Pets

Cats For Dummies,
2nd Edition
978-0-7645-5275-5

Dog Training For Dummies,
3rd Edition
978-0-470-60029-0

Puppies For Dummies,
2nd Edition
978-0-470-03717-1

Religion & Inspiration

The Bible For Dummies
978-0-7645-5296-0

Catholicism For Dummies
978-0-7645-5391-2

Women in the Bible
For Dummies
978-0-7645-8475-6

Self-Help & Relationship

Anger Management
For Dummies
978-0-470-03715-7

Overcoming Anxiety
For Dummies,
2nd Edition
978-0-470-57441-6

Sports

Baseball
For Dummies,
3rd Edition
978-0-7645-7537-2

Basketball
For Dummies,
2nd Edition
978-0-7645-5248-9

Golf For Dummies,
3rd Edition
978-0-471-76871-5

Web Development

Web Design
All-in-One
For Dummies
978-0-470-41796-6

Web Sites
Do-It-Yourself
For Dummies,
2nd Edition
978-0-470-56520-9

Windows 7

Windows 7
For Dummies
978-0-470-49743-2

Windows 7
For Dummies,
Book + DVD Bundle
978-0-470-52398-8

Windows 7 All-in-One
For Dummies
978-0-470-48763-1

Available wherever books are sold. For more information or to order direct: U.S. customers visit www.dummies.com or call 1-877-762-2974.
U.K. customers visit www.wileyeurope.com or call (0) 1243 843291. Canadian customers visit www.wiley.ca or call 1-800-567-4797.

Wherever you are in life, Dummies makes it easier.

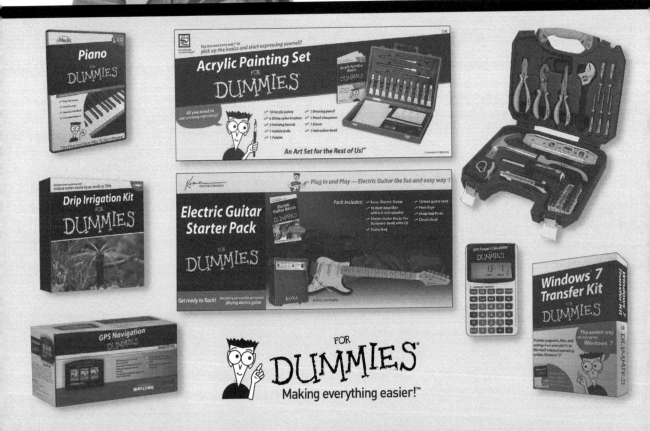

Made in the USA
San Bernardino, CA
15 March 2015